Financing Accounts Receivable for Retirement and Asset Protection

Financing Accounts Receivable for Retirement and Asset Protection

Ronald J. Adkisson

iUniverse, Inc.

New York Lincoln Shanghai

Financing Accounts Receivable for Retirement and Asset Protection

iUniverse books may be ordered through booksellers or by contacting:

iUniverse
2021 Pine Lake Road, Suite 100
Lincoln, NE 68512
www.iuniverse.com
1-800-Authors (1-800-288-4677)

ISBN-13: 978-0-595-37044-3 (pbk)
ISBN-13: 978-0-595-81447-3 (ebk)
ISBN-10: 0-595-37044-6 (pbk)
ISBN-10: 0-595-81447-6 (ebk)

Printed in the United States of America

Contents

Preface vii

Trademarks. xiii

Part I   *The Process*

CHAPTER 1   The Hidden Asset 5

CHAPTER 2   Transaction Economics 9

CHAPTER 3   Retirement Planning 14

CHAPTER 4   Asset Protection. 19

CHAPTER 5   Financing Under Fire 23

CHAPTER 6   The Players 25

CHAPTER 7   Tax Considerations 29

Part II   *Annuities*

CHAPTER 8   Introduction to Annuities 35

CHAPTER 9   Fixed and Single Premium Annuities. 42

CHAPTER 10   Equity Indexed Annuities (EIA) 45

Part III   *Life Insurance*

CHAPTER 11   Introduction to Life Insurance. 53

CHAPTER 12   Term Life Insurance 59

CHAPTER 13   Whole Life Insurance 62

CHAPTER 14   Universal Life Insurance 65

CHAPTER 15   Equity Indexed Life Insurance 68

Part IV   Other Considerations

CHAPTER 16   Structured Solutions 73

CHAPTER 17   Factoring 76

CHAPTER 18   Finding the Right Program for You 78

Additional Information 81

Lexicon 83

APPENDIX A   NAIC Consumer Alert: Tips for Buying Life
Insurance 99

APPENDIX B   NAIC Consumer Alert: Avoid Deceptive Sales
Practices 103

APPENDIX C   NASD Investor Alert: Equity Indexed
Annuities 107

APPENDIX D   Rule 11(d)(1) of the Securities Exchange Act of
1934 113

Preface

Accounts receivable (A/R) financing, which is simply borrowing against your unpaid invoices, has been around for ages. Its first cousin, the "factoring" of accounts receivables (which is their sale at a discount) has been around even longer. Both are long-established business strategies and a glance through the internet search engines reveals literally dozens of companies willing to give you money for your A/R on one basis or another.

What is new are the armies of insurance agents who are attempting to sell accounts receivable financing as an asset protection tool, primarily to physicians, in the hopes, of course, that the proceeds will be used to purchase an annuity or insurance product that will generate a commission. I don't begrudge them for this because fundamentally accounts receivable financing can be a good strategy when it is properly employed. The concern that I do have is that these agents are being sent out to sell complex A/R financing programs without any meaningful education or training about the numerous complex issues involved in these programs. To an extent, this book is for their education also.

The end result is that few insurance agents really understand what accounts receivable financing is all about or the impact it can have on your other estate and business planning, and their misperceptions might easily be passed along to you. Moreover, some A/R financing programs simply make no financial or legal sense, and a few make wild and highly questionable claims about tax benefits. It is too easy for you to get caught up in a bad program simply because its marketing materials were good and you had nothing to compare it against.

In any case, there simply is no resource about accounts receivable financing programs to review that will let you get a good understanding of the process and benefits, plus all the potential problems and pitfalls. Thus, I have written this book, which attempts to cover accounts receivable financing from the pre-loan strategy development, through the loan process and investment of the loan proceeds, and finally to the development of exit strategies, in a way which is hopefully readable and understandable by those who would consider these strategies.

An accounts receivable financing for retirement program appears to be a fairly simple arrangement on the surface. You leverage your accounts receivable by using it to collateralize a loan from a bank and use the borrowed funds to set something up for your retirement years. All you have to do is sign the papers and set back and let the program work for you. Right? But is that particular program right for your situation? Is it really the best solution for you?

My purpose for writing this book is not to answer those difficult questions for you because I don't know what your current situation is, what your other liabilities may be, what you may have already set-up for your retirement, or what your goals are. I don't even know if you are suitable for an accounts receivable financing program.

Suitability is stressed throughout this book. Suitability involves your personal risk tolerance, your financial situation, your other security holdings, your financial needs and your investment objectives. Probably the key component of suitability is that you fully understand what you are getting into. If you don't understand the program presented to you, then you are not suitable. Although your insurance agent has certain responsibilities to assure his recommendation is suitable for you, the decision to go forward resides in you alone. When you complete the reading of this book, my hope is that you will fully understand any accounts receivable financing plan presented to you.

Another issue that is stressed throughout this book is the need for you to seek competent counsel to help you incorporate an accounts receivable financing plan into your personal Big Picture. In addition to the liquidity, risk tolerance and suitability issues, there are other huge issues such as asset protection and taxes at play.

Asset protection is one of the best reasons to even look at accounts receivable financing; however, asset protection is a complex legal arena that requires a very high level of expertise. It is both dynamic, in that laws and regulations are constantly changing, and it is sometimes theoretical because some asset protection plans currently on the market have not yet been tested in court. It is a layered program that is at its best when coordinated with your business plans, your estate plans, your retirement plans, and other wealth management and generational plans which you have considered or should be considering. Any accounts receivable financing plan for retirement should be a part of your total asset protection program.

Resolving the tax issues is another area where outside help is required—unless you are already an expert. Taxes can make or break a financial program. It is too easy to be swayed by someone who uses the right buzzwords, speaks the language and, importantly, has great looking spread sheets that appear to add-up. The problem is: It is not that person who has to defend the program once you buy into it. At the end of the day, you are the one who has to defend your situation and pay any penalties that may be due. For my money, I would obtain a reputable tax counsel who will back me up if I have to stand in front of a judge and defend the program I bought into. There are too many downsides and it is worth a few bucks to sleep soundly at night.

Seek guidance! Don't try to do it yourself. Your lender is working for the lender and the insurance agent is working for the commission. The bottom line is that you are on your own. Seek guidance!

To help you understand accounts receivable financing and some of the buzz words you will hear during presentations, I have provided a summary of the process in Part I, which explains accounts receivables financing, asset protection, and tax issues involved. Part II provides a discussion of how annuities are used in A/R financing. Part III similarly provides information about life insurance products. Part IV offers a discussion about other structured solutions, factoring, and—most importantly—finding the program that is right for you.

To give you a little bit about your author, my career has been one continuous immersion in complex business transactions, mostly as an executive and consultant in the uranium mining and nuclear fuels fabrication industry. In later years, I obtained a life agent's license and then served in the capacity as an editor and advisor of the bestselling book on asset protection, "Asset Protection: Concepts and Strategies" by McGraw Hill & Company, by Jay Adkisson (my son) and Atlanta tax attorney Chris Riser. In assisting Jay with his practice, I have been involved in reviewing complex strategies that included exotic financial arrangements using annuities and life insurance products.

Accounts receivable financing will continue to grow in its use as a strategy for wealth creation and asset protection if for no other reason than that there are lenders, insurance agents, and program administrators who are pushing the concept hard. It is my hope that the expansion of the use of these programs be accompanied by careful thought and common sense in their development, which will only come about if the purchasers of these programs truly understand what they are all about and are able to intelligently compare the benefits and disadvantages of each program against the others. That is the understanding that I hope to impart by this book and I fervently hope that in the case of each reader that I will have succeeded in doing so in at least some significant part.

Acknowledgements

Several people helped immeasurably in bringing this book about. In a reversal of roles, Jay Adkisson acted as my editor and advisor as I had on his and Chris Riser's book. Chris and Joe Petrucelli, both of whose names are followed by the coveted LLM in tax law, contributed heavily in their thoughts on the tough tax issues. Investment advisors Tony Amaradio and Mark Goldsmith also made valuable contributions about the uses of annuities and life insurance products in these programs and about their economics.

Trademarks

As used herein:

"NASDAQ" is a registered trademark of the NASDAQ Stock Market, Inc.

"S&P 500" is a registered trademark of the McGraw-Hill Companies, Inc.

PART I
The Process

Accounts receivable financing is a relatively simple transaction. Basically, you are borrowing against your accounts receivable, taking the loan proceeds and making a distribution to yourself, and then investing the proceeds in a tax-deferred vehicle (usually an annuity or life insurance policy) that may be better protected from creditors than your accounts receivable would have been. Payment of the loan against your accounts receivables is guaranteed by a secured interest in the annuity or life insurance policy. Your business pays the lender interest while the loan is in place. You attempt to arbitrage the simple interest that you are paying annually on the loan against the compounded investment return that you will be earning in the annuity or life insurance product, or at least break even (in which case you should still get the substantial asset protection benefits).

This Part describes accounts receivable financing and why you would want to take a loan against your accounts receivable ("A/R") and invest the proceeds, and the ancillary benefits of that transaction.

Chapter 1—The Hidden Asset—Describes your accounts receivable and the financial reasons why you would want to borrow against it. Chapter 1 also offers an overview of accounts receivable financing programs.

Chapter 2—Transaction Economics—Discusses the economic underpinnings of these transactions and describes the arbitrage of simple versus complex interest. This chapter also warns about programs lacking in sound economics.

Chapter 3—Retirement Planning—The most popular end-goal of accounts receivable financing whereby you turn an underutilized asset into extra dollars for future use.

Chapter 4—Asset Protection—Tells why accounts receivable financing may help to deter lawsuits and facilitate settlements with creditors on more favorable terms. It also discusses the need to integrate other asset protection planning to make these programs work.

Chapter 5—Financing Under Fire—A candid discussion of what happens when creditors attempt to attack these programs and why the results may not always be as rosy as predicted by the promoters.

Chapter 6—The Players—This chapter discusses who-does-what in accounts receivable financing, what their interests are, and who (if anybody) is looking out for you.

Chapter 7—Tax Considerations—How these programs are taxed makes a very significant difference in how efficient they are. This chapter gives an overview of some of the most important tax issues.

1

The Hidden Asset

Accounts Receivable ("A/R") is a line item account on your company's balance sheet that summarizes the amount of money owed to you from the sale of your products or services, but for which you have not yet been paid. Underlying the balance sheet for your A/R are individual account ledgers for each customer that are usually supported by an invoice that details the product or service provided and the terms for their payment to you.

Until the invoice is paid it represents a loan from you to the customer. Instead of collecting cash from your customer at the time the service was provided or the product was delivered, you have invested your own cash in a loan to allow the customer time to remit the payment. You probably offer such credit primarily for the convenience of your customers or maybe for the benefit of third parties who will be paying the invoice on behalf of your customers, such as a medical insurance company. Customers clearly prefer to buy now and pay later in order to conserve their cash.

Yet, at the end of the day, you have still basically made a loan to your clients and their anticipated repayment to you is the asset which you book against the services or products sold. Thus, your accounts receivable is recorded on your balanced sheet as an asset. However, it is a "non-performing" asset. Your customers' promises to pay you in the near future still produces nothing for you today and you do not have access to their funds while their invoices are outstanding. In other words, your customers' promises to pay you are not something that you can take directly to the bank and deposit.

You can, however, either take a loan on your accounts receivable or sell your accounts receivable, which is what this book is all about.

A small firm's accounts receivable can be a large portion of their assets. For, example, it is not unusual for small companies, such as a medical clinic, to have an average of several hundred thousand or even a million dollars outstanding in accounts receivable throughout the year. Ironically, these uncollected assets are also very vulnerable assets that are exposed to a creditor's collections.

The accounts receivable can be used as collateral for a loan. Leveraging the use of the accounts receivable for collateral has been a fundamental form of lending for many years. It gives a company access to immediate cash while still waiting for clients to pay their invoices. It has been used to assist companies through a short-term cash crisis, to facilitate expansions, to restructure debt on more favorable terms, to pay taxes, and for a variety of other reasons. Indeed, borrowing against the accounts receivable is a well-grounded business strategy.

The way you need to think about the accounts receivable is as a "hidden asset" of your business. It is an asset that undeniably has some significant future value but is not being used. Your goal should be to think of ways to unlock this hidden asset, and reclaim its total value.

Accounts Receivable Financing does not involve the lender taking over the collection of your receivables. You will continue to collect the accounts and the cash stays in your business on a day-to-day basis. Your cash flow is not affected except for payments of the interest on the loan. Plans where the lenders take over the collection of receivables is called 'factoring' and is discussed in Chapter 16.

Banks want to expand their loan portfolios (*i.e.*, their own accounts receivable) to increase their profitability. This need of the bank to expand their loan business has caused them to create various specialty lending practices, including longer term accounts receivable financing. Not having enough of their own receivables to collect, they are willing to take over yours as well—and in a way you can both profit. Thus, many banks have developed specialized departments to evaluate your company's accounts and to lend your company funds based on the value of your accounts receivable.

What these banks look for is not a finite set of receivables, such as what you intend to collect from April to July. Instead, the banks are looking for long-term relationships whereby you are continually generating and collecting receivables and they are continually loaning you money based on those accounts. In many ways, you can think of it as a revolving credit arrangement where the credit extended to your company is backed by your company's accounts receivable. Such a relationship will require, of course, that your company be established, be fairly stable and that the probability that you will collect a certain percentage of your account receivables will be more-or-less predictable. Business or personal bankruptcy within the last 10 years or questionable solvency will probably disqualify an applicant from A/R financing.

During the life cycle of companies, once the start-up period ends, the accounts receivables begin to normalize. As the company matures, bad credit customers are being identified and eliminated and credit safeguards are being put into place to reduce the number of future non-paying customers. By this time, an accounts receivable collection history can be developed. Even if the company grows and increases its accounts receivable, the statistical performance of the account will remain fairly constant. At some point, the accounts receivables will become very predictable on an aggregate basis.

Ideally, 100% of the receivables would be paid within 10 days after receipt of the invoice. Sadly, that doesn't happen. Some customers will pay within 30 days, others within 60 days, and others may require a demand letter threatening collection before they get their checkbook out. As related earlier, there may also be third-party payers such as insurance companies who will require time to verify and process the claim before cutting a check. With good record-keeping, your business can develop a fairly predictable collection pro forma. The predictability of the accounts receivable, along with an evaluation of your customer portfolio and your company's collection practices, usually determines the "loanability" of your account receivables.

Keep in mind that as your business and your accounts receivable grow you are developing additional exposure for their value above the original loan amount. This means that you should review your accounts receivable periodically to expand your A/R financing and/or develop additional strategies to reduce that exposure. Accounts receivable financing should be a continually evolving strategy for your business, and not just a one-time transaction.

As discussed in Chapter 4 on Asset Protection, by using your accounts receivable as collateral for a loan, you have also removed the asset from the grasp of creditors since the bank would now stand ahead of any new creditors for the funds.

Once you have set it up with the bank and you have been declared "loanable", what do you do with the funds? Typically, the lender will insist that you put the funds into an investment such as an annuity or insurance product that the lender can take a security interest in as additional collateral for the loan (since it will be difficult for the lender to keep tabs on your A/R on anything like a daily basis). The most common types of products utilized are annuities and life insurance, which are discussed in Parts II and III of this book, although in Part IV we cover some alternative non-insurance strategies as well.

To develop an effective accounts receivable financing strategy, you must understand the economic theory that underlies these transactions—or else you may well find yourself in a transaction where you annually lose money. The next chapter discusses these economics.

2

Transaction Economics

The concept of compound interest plays an important role in accounts receivable financing transactions. Your economic goal is to successfully arbitrage the compounded interest you will generate on the loan proceeds against the simple interest you will pay on the loan. Over the long run you hope to make more with your investment of the loan proceeds, which will grow on a compounded basis, than you will pay out in simple interest to keep the loan alive.

The formula for compound interest is often stated as:

$$S = V(1 + i)^n$$

S = Final Value of the Investment
V = Initial Value of the Investment
i = Interest Rate
n = Number of Interest Periods

In accounts receivable financing you will use compound interest to grow what you borrow, which will theoretically grow at a faster rate than the simple interest you will pay on the loan against your accounts receivables. In other words, you are betting your long-term investment performance of the loan proceeds against the cost to maintain the loan. It is this arbitrage of compound interest versus simple interest that you are after, with your investment hopefully being tax deferred and your loan payments hopefully being currently deductible. See Chapter 7 on Taxes in Accounts Receivable Financing.

The loan to you is collateralized by both your investment and your accounts receivables, which should allow you to get a relatively low interest rate on that loan. Your goal then is to take this money and invest it for the highest return that you can get commensurate with the investment risks that you (and the lender which will have the financial product as collateral) are willing to accept.

Again, the loan you are taking will be repaid with "simple interest", but the product you purchase will pay "interest-on-interest" or compounded interest, meaning that it will build on itself each year whereas the former will not.

Most accounts receivable financing programs utilize life insurance or annuities as the funding mechanism. To a degree this is because these products are backed by the assets of large insurance companies, thus putting the lender at ease, but more importantly because these products have the advantage of growing tax-deferred.

For example, you can purchase a straight cash value life insurance (a "whole life policy") with a fixed compounded interest rate. Over the long term this will yield a higher net return than the interest paid on a simple interest loan. Why? Because every time interest is paid to the purchased product, the new interest calculation begins with the new balance. This works particularly well with products, such as an Equity Indexed Annuity (EIA), that offer opportunities to achieve higher gains through market movements while guaranteeing a minimum fixed interest rate. EIAs are discussed in Part II—Annuities.

Let's say, for example, that a total of $500,000 was borrowed on the basis of your accounts receivable. Let's assume the interest rate of this highly collateralized interest-only loan is 5% simple interest. Over a term of thirty years the interest on the loan would be $750,000 ($500,000 x .05 x 30 years). $500,000 earning an annual compounded rate of 5% over the thirty year period would return $2,160,971 resulting in a net overall gain of $910,971. Of course, some insurance products will be available to you that will yield substantially more than 5% compounded annually over a long period of time. A flat 5% simple interest loan rate is probably not realistic in today's market where long term variable rates are more likely to be offered but for our purposes we will assume a 5% simple interest rate.

Simple example of $500,000 loan:

Investment value using 5% compounded interest over 30 years	$2,160,971
Interest costs at 5% simple interest over 30 years	($750,000)
	========
Net investment value	$1,410,971
Repayment of loan	($500,000)
	========
Net Gain	$910,971

Actually, the simple interest and compound interest example above does not take into consideration a number of factors such as prime rate-based loan rates, potentially expensing the loan interest, or the advantages of deferring the tax on the compounded interest earned. A prime rate based loan floats with the changes in the rate moneys are loaned to banks by Uncle Sam. Banks tend to lower their prime rates when the federal government eases the money supply and they raise rates when the federal government contracts the money supply.

The built-in tax-deferral and the compounding of interest earned on those tax-deferred dollars within an insurance product are important components of the program. For example, had you put the above $750,000 total interest payments at the rate of $25,000 per year into an investment paying 5% interest compounded annually you would have paid Uncle Sam a total of $364,388, if you are in the 40% tax bracket. Within an insurance product, the tax is deferred and may even be protected from creditors in some states by statute.

Example of investing in a fixed interest vehicle:

Investment value of $25,000/year for 30 years at 5%	$1,660,971
Less Principal ($25,000 x 30 years)	($750,000)
	========
Total Gains	$ 910,971
Taxes at 40% payable as they are incurred	($364,388)
	========
Net Gain	$ 546,583

Additionally, if the loan repayment is deductible in your specific case, the actual interest cost to repay the loan would be much less. The ability for loan payments to be tax deductible is discussed in Chapter 16 on Structured Solutions.

If your loan qualifies for the tax deduction, the real dollar cost of the interest payments on the loan would be significantly less. You would have to pay the lender the same amount but the interest payments would be a deductible expense item which essentially excuses you from reporting that as income. Instead of making a $25,000 after tax payment, you would be making a $25,000 before tax payment or saving yourself the taxes on the amount. In the 40% tax bracket your real cost is $15,000 instead of $25,000. [$25,000 x (1-.40)]. Over the course of the 30 year period, the real dollar cost of paying the interest would be $450,000 instead of $750,000.

Example of deductible interest expense:

Investment value using 5% compounded interest over 30 years	$2,160,971
Interest cost at 5% simple interest over 30 years w/deductions	($450,000)
	========
Net Investment Value	$1,710,971
Repayment of loan	($500,000)
	========
Net Gain	$1,210,971

So, what have you accomplished? In this scenario you have basically just created an extra $1 million to add to your retirement by taking advantage of your hidden asset in your accounts receivable. But this isn't the only advantage to leveraging your receivables and in later chapters you will see why leveraging your accounts receivable provides you with significant non-financial benefits as well.

But Beware the Lost Opportunity Costs

Although it is possible to successfully arbitrage the compound interest that accrues within a tax-deferred investment against the simple interest paid on the loan, this is by no means a sure thing and many variables affect whether it works or not—particularly tax considerations as discussed in Chapter 7.

The opportunity cost that each program must be measured against is the calculation of how much money you would have made if you had not engaged in accounts receivable financing. This means that you take the amount of the interest payments that you would have made on the loan, distribute them to yourself and pay ordinary state and federal income taxes on those moneys, and then invest them in the very same financial product that you would have invested them in through the accounts receivable financing program.

Amazingly, many accounts receivable financing programs cannot beat this opportunity cost and, therefore, they do not make any economic sense! These programs may make sense for other reasons, such as to protect the A/R from creditors or to provide death benefits in the event the business owner dies, but from a purely number-crunching standpoint they do not make any sense at all. Indeed, with many programs A/R financing is a net loser and it would be an act of financial stupidity to engage in those programs (especially where better programs are available).

The bottom line is that in evaluating an accounts receivable financing program, you must ask your agent to run a lost opportunity analysis and compare it carefully against the benefits that you think that you will be getting. If economics are your only motivation for entering into the program, then those economics must be so significant as to make up for any restrictions that you may have in exiting the program, such as surrender charges in whatever product you end up investing in.

Sometimes accounts receivable financing makes sense because you will not take the money until retirement and then, presumably, at a lower tax bracket than when you were active in your business. In those situations, the difference in tax treatment might make the numbers look much better, as we will consider in the next chapter.

With some programs, it has not always been clear how the initial borrowed funds are repaid to the lender. This is an issue which they intentionally fudge or obscure, because their projections look much better without including the loan repayment. But even if they forget about it, your lender will not.

The note must be repaid and that repayment has to come either from the gains in the program, from the final uncollected receivables or from some other assets. In any case, the economic bottom line of your program will be substantially affected by the repayment of the loan, and there may be tax considerations as well. As you review a proposal, be sure to fully understand what the numbers represent in terms of paying back the loan and what the overall ramifications are to your bottom line.

3

Retirement Planning

One of the best uses of accounts receivable financing is to take this underutilized asset and unlock its full value into something that you can use to help seed your retirement funds. A good way to think of this is that you are "borrowing" your A/R from your business and then returning it to your business after some period of years—and keeping the investment growth to yourself.

When done correctly, accounts receivable financing for retirement basically works in the following steps:

1. You develop a comprehensive business, asset protection, and estate planning strategy that will encompass accounts receivable financing;

2. You obtain a simple loan from the bank using your accounts receivable as collateral, and you pay interest each year on the loan;

3. You then invest the funds into something that gives you compound interest and tax-deferred growth, which usually means an insurance product (i.e. annuity or life insurance), and which is protected from creditors;

4. When you sell or terminate your business or occupation, you repay the loan from the cash value of whatever you have invested in or from other assets; and,

5. You use the investment growth as part of your retirement nest-egg, taking it in years when you will possibly be in a lower income tax bracket.

The most important step is the first one, which is to develop a comprehensive strategy before you even begin. You simply must have a realistic and well-thought out game plan before you even begin this process.

Sadly, too many accounts receivable financing programs are set-up on a "Sign here and here" one-shot transactional basis where you may not fully realize what you have gotten into until you are well into it. This is not too much different than a first time pilot who launches himself into the sky only to then realize that he had never formulated a plan for landing. Rarely is there any need to rush into A/R financing.

The strategy that you develop must be a comprehensive beginning-to-end strategy that takes into account the totality of your business and personal planning. You absolutely must have a solid and well thought-out plan as to how your accounts receivable financing program will begin, operate, and terminate. The formulation of your plan must begin with a thorough review of your present situation and your long-term business and estate planning goals.

Integrating these plans and goals is typically something that will require the services of an experienced tax attorney. There are many reasons for this, but primarily it has to do with the overall tax efficiency of your arrangement and determining what may be tax-deductible or not. The economics of accounts receivable financing programs are primarily tax driven, which means that you must have a good tax attorney as your pilot.

How your particular plan is put together may also involve the question of what types of assets are exempted from creditors in your state. This is not a simple question that can be resolved by reference to a chart of state laws, since creditors' attorneys will "forum shop" for the jurisdiction most favorable to them and employ various strategies to attempt to circumvent your state's law. While your friendly insurance agent may be able to assist you with getting the best annuity or life insurance for your plan, it is dangerous to rely upon them for this extremely complex advice.

Suffice it to say that business and estate planning is an ongoing and dynamic process. Legislatures tend to change laws and personal situations tend to change during a person's lifetime. The development of a sound estate plan can mitigate the impact of any potential future change requirements by building in flexibility. By establishing a solid plan as your initial step, the inevitable business and personal changes that occur later can be more easily managed to your benefit.

By unlocking what was an underutilized asset, accounts receivable financing can provide funds that you can use to invest for your retirement goals. Even though you will ultimately have to repay the loan, in the interim you can benefit from the investment growth on the loan proceeds. Perhaps the best use of those moneys is to fund investments that will be used for retirement.

Why Life Insurance and Annuity Products Are Used

Although some people have an aversion to annuities and life insurance, they have several undeniable advantages over other investments. First, the investment growth within such products will often be tax-deferred. Second, the laws of some states have specific statutory exemptions for annuities and life insurance such that they cannot be attached by creditors (this is discussed in more depth in Chapter 4 on Asset Protection). Third, if life insurance is used it can be used to fund retirement, take care of the needs of the business owner's dependents, or even fund buy-sell arrangements if the business owner dies unexpectedly.

The primary reasons why you should use an insurance product to fund your retirement are:

1. tax-deferred growth within the policy;

2. access to tax-free loans, and in some cases withdrawal of funds, against the policy's cash value;

3. the power of compounded investment growth (see Chapter 2 on Transaction Economics); and,

4. financial protection for your dependents if you die unexpectedly.

If you are investing in life insurance purely for the tax-deferred growth, the calculation of whether you would use a particular life insurance product is the difference between your cost for the loan (the interest) and your anticipated investment gains within the insurance product. While the returns of an insurance product may not be as high as if you directly invested in a stock portfolio, you will not be paying capital gains or immediate income taxes on your investments and your investments would not provide for your premature death. Your stock portfolio would also present a tastier target for creditors to pursue since they generally have no exemption from attachment.

As discussed in Chapter 2 on Transaction Economics, placing the gains and tax deferrals on top of the premium payment and compounding the sum by each year's interest factor, results in exceptional growth of the cash value of the policy.

Various insurance products provide different methods to determine the interest rate paid by the policy. For example, a whole life insurance policy and a fixed annuity both offer a fixed rate of interest that will be assigned to the cash value each period. Other products offer the option of following a particular index, such as S&P-500, that allows you to participate in those gains. There are aggressive options and conservative options available, depending on your goals and risk tolerance. The options available to you are discussed in Part II, relating to Annu-ities, and Part III, relating to Life Insurance.

Risk tolerance and suitability issues are sometimes barely touched upon when discussing some insurance products. However, these are very important concepts which have a significant impact on your future. Be wary of any agent or planner who attempts to sell you something without discussing these issues with you very thoroughly.

One of the most delicate issues to consider is the issue of inflation. What will my money really be worth by the time I retire? Guaranteed interest rates of 3% or 5% don't sound very exciting if you consider a future with high inflation. Additionally, your investment performance within these products will have to exceed the amount you are paying on the A/R financing loan for these programs to make any sense. So, you have to ask the question of how much of your loan proceeds are you willing to risk to invest in other potentially higher gain options.

You must also consider that as your business grows and your A/R grows respectively, you may wish to consider additional loans. Another issue is that as the years go by the current loan will also have "shrunk" in terms of future dollars. The upshot of all this is that your A/R financing plan must be periodically reeval-uated to make sure that it still fits you well.

Developing Your Exit Strategy

Companies may last forever—indeed, some states now allow some forms of busi-ness entities to last in perpetuity—but you aren't going to. Sooner or later you will have to develop an exit strategy for yourself from your business, or at least a succession plan to pass your business on to whomever.

Developing and implementing an exit strategy is important. If you own a business, what are your plans for the business when you decide to retire? There are tax consequences if you sell it, if you hand it down, and even if you just close the doors and go home.

In the normal course of business, when that time comes you will still have some catching up to do as far as your accounts receivables are concerned. When a business stops and there continues to be outstanding receivables, the period to collect these outstanding receivables is called the "runoff period". One alternative is to use some or all of the receivables collected during the runoff period to repay the loan. Another alternative may be to pay the loan from the proceeds of the investment vehicle you chose (i.e. give back the amount you borrowed and keep the gains). But these alternatives may not be best for you.

For example, because of extra cash availability during the operation of the business you may decide to pay back the loan (i.e. make an interest and principle payment to pay down the loan) and keep the total investment for retirement but keep in mind that as you pay down the loan, you are increasing your exposure to creditors. If you sell the business you can take part of the proceeds to repay the loan or you may have other assets to use to repay the loan at the appropriate time.

There are a number of ways to go about this and, again, the assistance of a knowledgeable tax planner should be involved in the planning stage. Together you can determine what best suits your particular situation to exit the business in the most tax advantaged way for you and to build-in the proper mechanisms in the event you change your mind 15 years down the road.

The Bottom Line

Using your accounts receivable for financing retirement by converting a currently non-productive asset into a productive asset can be a good thing for you in the right circumstances. Keep in mind, however, that it is just one tool towards developing an overall plan which includes your retirement, your overall estate planning, your wealth accumulation and, possibly, other generational issues. With proper planning, accounts receivable financing can be a very important tool for your retirement years.

However, you must be aware that sometimes the economics of A/R financing programs simply do not work out, or are marginal. In these cases, you will have to weigh other considerations to decide whether to implement such a program. The most important "other consideration" is often asset protection, which we will discuss next.

4

Asset Protection

Your accounts receivable offers one of the easiest assets that creditors will be able to collect upon. The creditor need only attach your accounts receivable and then cash the checks as they come in. This is easy money for a creditor.

The large build-up in your accounts receivable makes you a correspondingly larger target for lawsuits. Creditors will be less likely to consider a cheap settlement if they know that they can collect against your personal and business assets. Your business assets include your accounts receivable, and a creditor will hope that your A/R will be available to fund the creditor's chase for other assets. In other words, leaving your accounts receivable exposed to creditors gives them the opportunity to use your accounts receivable to fund their fight to break the protections of your other assets.

It is critically important that protecting your accounts receivable be an integral part of your risk management and asset protection planning. The best way to protect your accounts receivables is simply to borrow against them so that there is no equity left for creditors to get. This is a practice known as Equity Stripping, and it has a high chance of success so long as it is done well in advance of any claims arising.

Since the lender will place a UCC-1 lien on your accounts receivable, the lender will always be first in-line to collect those assets. The creditor will presume that you will simply default on the loan, and the lender will foreclose on your accounts receivable to satisfy your loan obligation. This will close out the loan and, more importantly, leaves little or nothing for creditors to collect.

Borrowing against your accounts receivable should not be considered a fraudulent transfer since you receive something back for allowing the lender to place the UCC-1 lien, which was the loan. This means that the transaction should be considered a *bona fide* for-value transaction and the creditor's remedy is not against the lender or your accounts receivable but rather against the loan proceeds that you received.

This brings us to the second part of the asset protection equation: How do you protect the loan proceeds from creditors?

Many strategies have been devised over the years to protect liquid assets, such as these loan proceeds, from creditors. Attempting to list and describe each and every strategy is well beyond the scope of this book. Suffice it to say that some strategies are more solid and have met with better success than other strategies, so we will only discuss a few of the major ones here.

At the outset, you should understand that asset protection planning is typically done in layers. It is also done in a fail-safe fashion so that if one layer fails, the assets will still be protected by another layer. Because of this, the asset protection strategies discussed below are often used in tandem with at least one other strategy.

We have already discussed that it makes financial sense to invest the loan proceeds into an annuity or life insurance because of the ability to have tax-free or tax-deferred investment growth. It also makes asset protection sense to invest in these types of products. There are several reasons for this but the primary reason is that annuities and life insurance give indigestion to creditors.

The reason for this indigestion deals with state protections for life insurance and annuities. Some states protect these products from creditors completely, other states protect them if they are structured in certain ways, and other states protect them in substantial part. Where these protections exist, they are effective even in bankruptcy court and are almost impossible for creditors to get around. Years of case law has established the asset protection benefits of annuities and life insurance in those states where they are protected in whole or in part.

Even in the few states where they are not protected from creditors at all, it is often difficult for creditors to get at the value in these products for jurisdictional and procedural reasons. The creditor also risks that between the time the lawsuit is commenced and the creditor attempts collection, the debtor will have moved to a state where annuities and life insurance are fully protected. Annuities and life insurance are thus much less attractive to creditors than a big pile of cash waiting to be collected, which is essentially what your accounts receivable are.

In some states you can accomplish the same asset protection goal by putting the funds from your accounts receivable financing into your house. But it makes absolutely no financial sense to do this. Your home will appreciate at the same rate whether it is 10% paid off, 50% paid off, or 100% paid off. This means that having equity in your home is "dead equity" that is not working for you. By contrast, having your money in an annuity or life insurance policy will give you the investment returns that you need to make the arrangement work out financially.

Another strategy involves contributing the loan proceeds from your accounts receivable financing to a Limited Liability Company (LLC) or Limited Partnership (LP) through which you invest in other ventures. The idea is that you have transformed liquid cash into an illiquid investment interest. While this can financially work if the entity's investments succeed, it might be weighed down by the tax liability that will be distributed to you every year from the entity. Also, there will be costs associated with maintaining the entity and associated structuring costs with its management which must be considered. Finally, it can be difficult to find a lender who will go along with such an arrangement.

Perhaps a better arrangement is to use the funds as an investment into what is known as a "Beneficiary Taxed Irrevocable Trust" (BETIR Trust, pronounced "Better Trust"). This is a trust that is set up for you by some third person (such as your parent or sibling) with you as the beneficiary. Typically, the trust will be a grantor trust, meaning that all income tax consequences will flow through to you. Once you have transferred money into the trust, these moneys and the asset(s) that they have purchased should be shielded from your creditors by the trust's spendthrift provisions, and later even from your children's creditors. These trusts can also resolve estate planning and succession issues when you die as well as take care of your spouse, if necessary.

An ideal structure would involve the sale of the proceeds from your accounts receivable financing into a BETIR Trust and then having the BETIR Trust purchase either annuity or life insurance products, depending on your financial need. In the event of your death, the policy proceeds from a life insurance policy would stay in the BETIR Trust for the benefit of your heirs. The proceeds would also be shielded from your heirs' future creditors as well.

In the case of annuities, the BETIR Trust would provide you with access to a retirement stream that creditors would not be able to access. Moreover, because of some states' exemptions for annuity and life insurance products, creditors might be deterred from even attempting to get at these assets inside the trust.

There are many other asset protection strategies that can be employed to protect the loan proceeds from your accounts receivable financing program. The best strategy for you will depend on the particulars of your situation. You must avoid using a "canned" or one-size-fits-all arrangement that is proposed to you by the A/R financing company or by the insurance agent who is designing a product for you. Instead, you should take the time to have an attorney, familiar with asset protection planning issues, custom design a plan for your specific circumstances and needs.

One such firm that I often work closely with in these matters is the law firm of Riser Adkisson LLP. You'll recognize the last name as that of my son, Jay Adkisson, who is nationally known as one of the leading commentators on asset protection planning issues. Jay, along with his law partner, Chris Riser, have written an excellent treatise on the subject: *Asset Protection: Concepts and Strategies*, which is published by McGraw-Hill & Company. This highly-recommended book is available at most Barnes & Nobles and Borders stores and is available online at *http://amazon.com*. Likewise, they maintain an extensive website on asset protection issues, including a free newsletter, at *http://www.assetprotectionbook.com*

In the next chapter, we will see how accounts receivable financing programs stand up—and sometimes don't stand up—when challenged by creditors.

5

Financing Under Fire

So far, we have discussed the economics of accounts receivable financing and talked about how the asset protection benefits are supposed to work. But what happens if a creditor gets a judgment against your business and attempts to collect on your A/R?

The creditors' success will depend on many things, including how sophisticated and determined the creditor is. If the creditor is lazy or unsophisticated, the creditor may see the UCC-1 lien on the receivables and conclude that there is nothing for the creditor to get. Such a creditor may move on to pursue other less-protected assets, or perhaps even another case. This, many attorneys predict, will probably occur most of the time or, at least, until A/R financing becomes better known by collection attorneys.

But what if the creditor is sophisticated and determined? In this event, the creditor will still not be able to get at the present value of the accounts receivable. What the creditor might do, however, is to go ahead and foreclose on your A/R even if there is no current value in your A/R for the creditor to get. Although foreclosure is an expensive and time consuming process, this will force your lender to immediately collect its loan against your receivables. When your lender is paid off, the lender's UCC-1 lien will disappear and whatever future A/R that your business generates will become available to creditors. What this means is that you will either have to stop doing business or you will just be working for the creditor until the judgment is paid off.

This is one of the hidden, dirty secrets of A/R financing that many promoters will not disclose to you. Although the creditor will not get any value out of your accounts receivable, the creditor will effectively have put an end to your business.

In some circumstances you might not care, especially if the litigation has wrecked the business anyway, but in other circumstances, such as an ongoing professional practice, this creates a situation as difficult for you as it is for the creditor. The most likely outcome here is settlement on terms that are satisfactory or unsatisfactory, depending on how you look at it, to both you and the creditor.

Some promoters might tell you something like, "Well, if that happens, you can just start a completely new business and start collecting your A/R in that new business." While that may sound good to you, in reality the courts are likely to apply some theory such as successor corporation liability or fraudulent transfer law to deem your new corporation to simply be an extension of your old one for collection purposes (its not like you will have been the first debtor ever to attempt that maneuver).

The other situation that you have to look out for is if you and your business get sued and the creditor is able to freeze all your bank and financial accounts. This might prevent you from coming up with money to service your loan, meaning that your lender will then exercise its security right against your collateral—usually meaning whatever financial product you have purchased, since your lender doesn't really want to be in the business of actually having to collect your receivables. This would be the nightmare scenario, since not only would you lose your financial product but when the lender is paid off it would also expose your A/R to you creditors (presuming that they could use their judgment against you to penetrate your business structure to get at its assets).

The key to avoiding all these scenarios is advanced asset protection planning such as making sure that you will have a source of funding the interest payments so there is never a default. We have repeatedly emphasized that advanced planning is the key to making accounts receivable financing work in real-world litigation and we emphasize it again here. You simply cannot allow yourself to be placed into a "canned" A/R financing program without the necessary asset protection planning or you will have accomplished nothing if a sophisticated and determined creditor comes along.

6

The Players

One of the most common errors committed by businessmen who get into accounts receivable financing programs is that they do not understand—at all—who represents their interests in these transactions. The answer is: Nobody!

In this transaction there are three separate but closely related players who will put the plan together for you—the lender, the insurance agent and the program administrator.

The lender represents itself. The lender's primary desires are that it has a contractual right to interest payments and is adequately secured both by the receivables and by other collateral. The "other collateral" often means whatever insurance product is purchased with the funds from the transaction. Generally, the lender will allow you to borrow somewhere between 80% to 100% of your accounts receivables which they may calculate from an average of your A/Rs over a period of time, or a high water mark during a period. The interest rate charged by the lender is generally a variable rate that can be the prime rate offered to secured banks plus a percentage, LIBOR, or another variable rate measuring program. The rate actually charged may depend on your credit score.

The lender may not care what the product you purchase is, so long as the product will be good collateral for the loan. Nor will the lender care whether you, as the borrower, are protected in any way. Lenders may have a marketing interest in seeing that you are generally happy so that they get more business, but legally they owe you absolutely no legal obligations whatsoever other than to adequately disclose to you the terms of their loan.

The next player is the insurance agent. Odds are that it was an insurance agent who told you about this deal and it is no secret that the insurance agent's goal is the commission from whatever product you buy with the proceeds from the loan. We don't begrudge the agent this interest since, after all, if the program works then it was a pretty good idea that he or she brought to you.

Just keep in mind that the insurance agent is not necessarily looking out for your best interests in this transaction. Although state insurance laws impute some duties to the insurance agent to protect you as to the insurance side of the transaction, the insurance agent owes you absolutely no duties whatsoever to make sure that the financing side of the transaction is in your best interests.

Even if the insurance agent was trying to look out for your interests, he or she is probably ill-equipped to do so. Insurance agents are not typically trained in these types of transactions and what little education they may receive about them is almost exclusively provided by the lenders. Of course, the lenders are not going to go out of their way to tell the insurance agents what they should be looking out for in these transactions and the insurance agents often have scarcely any familiarity with Uniform Commercial Code finance law.

The last player is the program administrator or "facilitator" or whatever you wish to call the third group. The program administrator is a professional company that specializes in accounts receivable financing. They are usually heavily tied to a lender and generally earn a portion of their fees in the form of the spread on the loan and a percentage of the insurance product. For example, the program facilitator may add 0.5 to 2% to the loan rate.

The program administrator qualifies the borrower, provides the calculated pro forma detail which shows the costs and projected outcomes of the program, and generally acts on behalf of the lender to structure and consummate the program. The insurance agent is active with the program administrator to put together the deal by providing an insurance product for which the agent receives the commission. But at the end of the day, the program administrator's main job is marketing the program to insurance agents to sell to people like you, and in processing paperwork. They owe you no legal duties to look out for your interests, either.

So, who looks out for you in these transactions? Nobody!

This is why it is critically important that you retain an attorney to represent your interests and make sure you are protected on the financing side. There are very important aspects to these accounts receivable financing transactions that your lender will never tell you about and your insurance agent probably will not catch where your attorney probably would. Additionally, as emphasized repeatedly throughout this book, for these programs to really work against a determined creditor there must be some other asset protection structure, which only attorneys are qualified and experienced to properly implement.

Some of the issues an attorney would be able to identify and assist you with include such items as:

- Most accounts receivable financing programs include callable loans. Therefore, the product you purchase with the funds needs to have cash value liquidity or you need to have other cash available to repay the loan.

- Some plans may charge a fee for paying off the loan early which could be a problem under any number of different circumstances.

- Since the interest rates are variable and may or may not have a cap, it is a good reason to use the funds to purchase a product with more than a fixed rate of return, such as an Equity Indexed Annuity. It is important that you be prepared to repay the loan and cancel the arrangement if the interest rate goes too high.

- Some program administrators will not accept sole proprietorships or general partnerships for their accounts receivables financing plans. These structures are not good asset protection structures anyway and it may make sense to restructure your business to make accounts receivable financing work efficiently.

- If one professional in a practice group, but not all professionals within the group, desires to engage in accounts receivable financing, the accounts receivables of the one professional can be carved out and separately protected.

There is another reason why it is critically important that you have your own attorney represent you in these transactions: attorney-client privilege.

Your communications with the lender will never be protected by attorney-client privilege nor will your communications with your insurance agent or program administrator. If you tell any of these, for instance, that the purpose of your engaging in accounts receivable financing was for asset protection purposes because of potential lawsuits, then you have put the entire arrangement at risk. The lender, the insurance agent, and the program administrator can all be subpoenaed and forced under penalty of contempt to testify as to this conversation—which could potentially unwind the transaction as a fraudulent transfer (because of the stated intent to lessen the ability of creditors to collect).

By contrast, your discussions with your attorney will normally be protected by attorney-client privilege and you can speak with him or her candidly about what you are trying to accomplish. Your attorney can then carefully review the transactional documents to make sure that your goals are being met and that you will not receive any nasty surprises later. Your attorney can also implement the necessary asset protection planning (if they practice in that area, but caution that few attorneys do) to give you the highest level of confidence that your A/R financing arrangement will work as you intended for it to work.

More importantly, you will need an attorney to help you navigate the critically important, numerous and hazardous tax issues involved with accounts receivable financing, as will now be discussed.

7

Tax Considerations

The tax issues involved with accounts receivable financing can be very complex. Among the issues to be considered in evaluating the efficiency of any particular program are loan interest deductions, the taxation of the distributions of loan proceeds, the tax issues involved in settling up between the business and a retiring owner, the taxation of income and gains earned inside the insurance or annuity product, and the taxation of distributions or loans from the insurance or annuity product to the owner.

You must fend for yourself when it comes to tax issues. The lender won't care and the insurance agent won't be qualified to give tax advice. The program administrator may provide some general information, and may offer a copy of a memo or tax opinion written by a law firm for the administrator for their benefit. However, you can't rely on a tax opinion to avoid penalties assessed by the IRS unless certain conditions are met, one of which is that the opinion is addressed to you specifically.

So, as the program administrator probably will advise you to do, seek your own separate tax advice to specifically address your situation. This is the only way to get comfortable with the tax issues particular to you. Furthermore, a business and tax attorney reviewing your situation likely will be able to identify other areas for business and financial improvement.

Following is a brief overview of some of the tax issues involved in accounts receivable financing. The purpose of this overview is merely to alert you to these issues, not to solve the issues or suggest a probable outcome. The tax issues will vary from program to program and from participant to participant.

Loan Interest Payments

The issue upon which many potential participants focus is the deductibility of loan interest payments. One thing is clear—if the individual participant is the borrower, the interest is not deductible. If the business is the borrower, the issue is murky at best. However, an accounts receivable financing program will rarely make financial sense if the interest is not deductible. The program may make sense for other reasons, such as removing your accounts receivable from the easy reach of business creditors, but it will rarely make financial sense.

So, when might interest payments be deductible?

The promoters of these programs claim that the interest payments might be deductible business expenses if the arrangement is structured correctly. The key here is to recognize that there are several tax issues at work and not just the one regarding interest. If all your business did was to leverage its accounts receivable for some purely business purpose, such as to purchase equipment or maybe just to increase available liquidity, it would be much more likely that the interest payments would be deductible for your business.

Difficult questions arise when the proceeds from accounts receivable financing directly or indirectly are put to personal use, such as the purchase of a life insurance or annuity product. The issue isn't simply the deductibility of the interest, but rather how the loan proceeds get to the owner.

A similar question involves whether the loan against the accounts receivable is even necessary at all since the lender will be fully secured by the life insurance or annuity product. If the receivables really don't seem to be at risk of being liquidated to pay back the loan, the loan—at least with respect to the business and its receivables—may seem less like a business loan and more like a personal loan.

This risk is heightened for programs that are designed so that the lender is 100% secured by the financial product into which the loan proceeds are invested, although it may depend on the language of the loan documents and whether the business owner is acting in the role of a guarantor of the loan. Whether a program is "with recourse" or "without recourse" might make a dramatic difference when it comes to tax treatment.

Distribution of the Loan Proceeds

Some promoters claim that if the business is taxed as a pass-through entity (i.e., as an S corporation or partnership), it may be possible to avoid income taxes on the distribution of the loan proceeds to the owner. The transfer of the loan proceeds to the owner generally is a deductible expense for an S corporation (and, generally, is a non-event for a partnership, for practical purposes). Since there is no corresponding income to offset that expense in an S corporation, a loss passes through to the owner, which would generally offset the income received by the owner from the distribution of the loan proceeds. However, tax laws require that an S corporation shareholder have "basis" in his shares at least equal to the amount of the loss in order to use the loss that is passed through. Many share-holders may not have enough basis to use the loss, and thus would have taxable income—perhaps up to the full amount of the distributed loan proceeds—but without receiving an additional distribution of cash to pay the taxes owed.

Things get very complicated for tax purposes when less than all of the owners of a business participate in the program. A business taxed as a partnership likely can work out a solution acceptable to the non-participating owners. However, a business taxed as an S corporation likely will have a difficult time working out a solution because of the restrictions on S corporation flexibility contained in the tax laws. Highly competent tax advice is a must.

Mirror Loans

Other promoters suggest that the business should lend the loan proceeds to the owner instead of making a one-time compensation payment. Such loans some-times are called "mirror loans" because the lender makes a loan to the business, which then makes a loan of the same funds to the owner. While this may avoid tax on the transfer from the business to the owner, it implicates other tax issues related to the loan between the business and the owner. Again, these are issues requiring highly competent tax advice.

Recourse Financing: The Basis Boost

Some promoters claim that if the business is taxed as a partnership, an interesting opportunity may arise if the owners guarantee the business loan. To the extent that a partner is at risk economically for the debt of the partnership, the partner's income tax basis in his ownership interest is increased. You might conceptualize it as being similar to the partner actually contributing cash to the partnership. Because withdrawals from a partnership are tax-free to the extent of the partner's basis, the partner may be able to avoid tax consequences on the distribution of the loan proceeds from the business.

Although it may be an easy solution at the inception of the program, it may come back to haunt the owner at termination, when the loan payoff reduces his basis or causes him to have taxable income with no corresponding additional dis-tribution of funds to pay the tax. Again, repeat the mantra: These are issues requiring highly competent tax advice.

Too Good To Be True?

At the extreme end of the aggressive scale, some accounts receivable financing programs purportedly are designed to generate a substantial deduction to the business for the amount financed. The tax authority upon which these programs are based is highly suspect. At best, it is likely that the deduction would be denied, with the owner owing the tax, plus interest and perhaps penalties. At worst, the program would be deemed a tax shelter and the deduction would be denied; the owner would owe tax, interest and stiff penalties; and, the promoters and others involved in the marketing of the program may be subject to penalties, or worse.

This is a particular risk when the promoter claims to have a patented or proprietary product, and requires the signing of non-disclosure agreements. Under new laws meant to discourage tax shelters, the fact that a program is claimed to be proprietary puts it a step closer to abusive tax shelter treatment. Note that opinion letters issued to the promoters are probably worthless to avoid penalties if it is later deemed to be a tax shelter.

Beware of promoters promising large tax deductions with their accounts receivable financing arrangements. Seek the independent advice of a qualified tax attorney who has no relationship with the promoters. If the promoters tell you not to seek such a second opinion or require that your tax attorney sign a non-disclosure agreement (which may be ethically improper for the attorney), then your course is clear: Run!

In Summary

A business owner contemplating an accounts receivable financing program must hire a qualified tax attorney to review the transaction's validity and to ensure that there are no hidden tax traps for the business owner. Moreover, the attorney may be able to spot other tax and business planning opportunities for the business that would make the use of accounts receivable financing even more advantageous. As suggested throughout, accounts receivable financing should be part and parcel of an overall business and asset protection planning strategy, and not a one-off or stand-alone transaction.

PART II
Annuities

Annuities are made for retirement planning, which fits them in perfectly with many accounts receivable financing programs. This Part discusses annuities in general and then concentrates on the type of annuities that are most commonly used in conjunction with accounts receivable financing.

Chapter 8—Introduction to Annuities—An overview of what annuities are, and how they are used in both general financial planning and in accounts receivable financing programs.

Chapter 9—Fixed and Single Premium Annuities—Forms of annuities with fixed rates of return that may either start immediately or defer their payout until some future date.

Chapter 10—Equity Indexed Annuities—The most popular annuity for use with accounts receivable financing is safe, efficient, and sometimes very difficult to understand.

Please note that we will not be discussing Variable Annuities which, as their name suggests, vary with the stock markets—down as well as up. This risk of loss of principal is too great for most A/R lenders to even consider accepting them as collateral. High internal fees and Rule 11(d)(1) of the Securities Act of 1934 also present significant deterrence against their use in the accounts receivable financing context.

8

Introduction to Annuities

In its most basic form, an annuity is something that you buy now that will make a stream of payments until your death. Whereas other investments will end on a given future date, an annuity will keep paying you money no matter how long you live. As opposed to a life insurance policy that protects your heirs from your premature death, the purpose of an annuity is to financially protect you in case you live too long—and also, of course, to provide retirement benefits along the way.

Like any competitive product, there are many variations to the basic form of annuities. Later chapters will discuss several of the more important variations as they relate to accounts receivable financing.

Since the insurance company cannot tell in advance who will live at what age, the insurance company employs the "Law of Large Numbers" to actuarially guess at what age most people in certain categories will die. The insurance company can't predict with much accuracy when a particular annuitant will die, but it can make a pretty accurate average prediction on when 10,000 people will die.

Even if you live past your life expectancy, the insurance company is still on the hook and must make annuity payments to you no matter how long you live. So, if your life expectancy is 78 and you actually live until the age of 99, the insurance company has to make annuity payments to you through all those extra years. Again, annuities protect you from the financial uncertainty of living too long.

Because of this ongoing obligation of the insurance company to make annuity payments no matter how long you live, annuities are perhaps the single best retirement vehicle that you can buy. Especially with improvements in healthcare and elder care causing most people to live longer, their immediate fear is not so much death, as it is outliving their retirement. Thus, the use of annuities has substantially grown in recent years and is expected to become much greater as the baby boomers start retiring.

Another way to look at this is that life insurance creates an asset (a pool of money for your heirs), whereas an annuity liquidates an asset for your retirement. You create a future asset with life insurance by periodically putting money into the contract, i.e., build it up over a period of years. To the converse, an annuity's function is to liquidate the contract that you have purchased by continually taking money out of it. The goal of a life insurance policy is to have a lot of money in it at your death; whereas, the goal of an annuity is to have nothing in it at your death.

Annuities are not life insurance policies. Life insurance pays cash benefits when you die. Annuities typically begin paying income when you retire and may pay you for as long as you or your spouse may live. It is a contract between you and an insurance company.

Why an insurance company? The function of guaranteeing annuity payments for many people who will all have varying and unpredictable life spans, is very much an insurance function. Besides, what other type of entity keeps the tightly-regulated reserves and financial strength that insurance companies have such that they can guarantee income for the rest of your life?

Mechanics

In an annuity, you (the "annuitant") agree to pay the insurance company either a single payment or a series of payments and the insurance company agrees to pay you an income for a specified period of time—usually, but not always, until your death. The money you put into an annuity is your money and is not taxed when it is returned to you. Earnings or gains are taxed when paid to you through withdrawals or through periodic payments. With the compounding of tax-deferred earnings and gains, the funds will typically grow at a faster pace than most fixed income instruments.

With the exception of the so-called Single Premium Immediate Annuity (SPIA), that starts paying you immediately after you purchase it, there are usually two phases to an annuity: Accumulation and Annuitization.

Accumulation is the process of funding the annuity or building it up so it will pay you later. The period during which you build up the annuity and before you start taking payments is called the "accumulation period". The funds grow with interest and/or investment earnings during the accumulation period.

Annuitization means that you have started your annuity and payments will now be made to you until the end of your life. In other words, the funds that you have accumulated are now ready for your withdrawal and distribution to you or the start of payments to you.

In practice it seems that few people actually have the insurance company start making payments to them, but instead will withdraw the money from the policy and make another investment. This occurs because at that point in time they have determined that their other sources of income will take care of them, and they want to keep deferring their payments until some future date. So, they will roll their annuity over to another investment as allowed by the tax laws, often to another annuity.

In both the accumulation and annuitization phases you have lots and lots of options. Some of these options are common to all annuities while others are specific to certain products. But with most decisions to purchase an annuity, you will be faced with the following questions:

- How will you fund the annuity?

- What investments do you wish the annuity to invest in until you annuitize?

- Will you need access to your funds?

- How will you want the annuity to pay out to you?

Funding Your Annuity

In considering how you fund your annuity, you have two options. You can make a one-time lump sum payment. This would be useful if you wanted to convert a large sum of cash or convert your life insurance policy or your IRA to an annuity. Under the 1035 exchange rules, a life insurance contract can be exchanged for an annuity on a tax-free basis; however, the converse is not true since an annuity cannot be tax-free exchanged for a life insurance policy. If you fund your annuity with a one-time lump-sum payment it is known as a "single premium annuity".

Your second option involves making periodic payments over time to create an investment fund that will later be used to determine what your annuity payments will be. The best way to look at this is that you are creating a fund that you will later use to purchase the annuity payments, although your funding will be considered part of the annuity contract (so that your money in the annuity contract qualifies for tax-deferred growth). In other words, you are effectively deferring the time when your annuity will start, which is why such an annuity is called a "deferred annuity".

Usually, a deferred annuity works by giving you "accumulation units" based on how much money you invest and how good the investment performance of the contract was prior to annuitization. When you decide to annuitize, the amount of your annuity payments will be based on how many accumulation units your contract has earned. Again, it's like saving up your money to buy an annuity later but the annuity contracts go through this façade of the accumulation units to satisfy our kindly friends at the IRS that the growth really is in an annuity contract (and not just a disguised mutual fund) and thus should be tax-deferred.

Investment Options

The consideration of investment options is where the process of selecting an annuity becomes more difficult, but the bottom line is: How much risk are you willing to assume? You can contract an annuity with a relatively low fixed guaranteed interest rate or you can shoot for much higher earnings by investing in an annuity that has an investment method that is tied to stock market performance. There are several ways to test your risk tolerance between these two extremes.

Risk tolerance and suitability are terms that you will see often in this book. Older folks close to retirement may not wish to risk a lot of money and may, therefore, desire the security of a fixed interest rate. Younger folks with the ability and time to stay the course may desire to maximize their potential earnings by selecting a higher risk investment strategy that tracks the stock market. Then, of course, there are many options in between.

Accessing Your Funds

Access to funds is a big issue when discussing annuities. Although most deferred annuities offer you a cash value that you can withdraw, your ability to withdraw might be restricted by surrender charges, which are basically penalties for early withdrawal. Surrender charges vary greatly from product to product. Some products have little or no surrender charges, while other products have very steep surrender charges. There may also be other contractual provisions which could limit your ability to withdraw from or cash-out of your policy.

Surrender charges and restrictions on withdrawals serve the purpose of the insurance company in encouraging you to keep your money in your policy. But in many ways, this serves your interests also in making you view your annuity as a very long-term investment instead of a short-term stock portfolio account that you can dip into willy-nilly whenever you want to buy a car or go on a cruise, etc. Remember, its ultimate purpose is to fund your retirement until your hopefully distant death.

The real question is not whether you will frivolously want your money or not, but whether you will potentially need it during the surrender period. If you suspect that you might need to access the money in the annuity during the surrender period, which is often years 1 through 15, then the annuity is not suitable for you and you should avoid it. So, you shouldn't be putting into the annuity any money that you might need returned during the surrender period. If any insurance agent tries to convince you to still invest in the annuity in spite of this potential need, then you need a new insurance agent for such practices are illegal. Again, annuities are long-term vehicles to fund retirement all the way until your death. They are not short-term piggybanks for rainy days or monthly financial crunches.

Uncle Sam encourages investments in annuities as retirement vehicles by offering tax-deferral on gains earned inside the annuity. But Uncle Sam also taketh away if you withdraw funds before retirement. A 10 percent penalty tax is imposed on withdrawals from a deferred annuity before age 59 ½. Withdrawals after age 59 ½ are not subject to the 10 percent penalty tax but any gains are taxed as ordinary income. Partial withdrawals are treated first as earnings income before they are treated as a return on principal.

Annuitization

The annuitization date is the date on which your annuity will start making payments to you. Some annuity contracts require that you specify this date in advance. Others give you the choice of waiting to annuitize until you need the payments to begin. It is known as an 'immediate annuity' if the annuity starts paying immediately after you purchase it.

Most people will fund the annuity while they are working and then start to withdraw shortly after retirement to make up for their lower retirement income. What strategy you have for funding your annuity and then starting the annuity payments will be important for determining the type of annuity to best fit you. Often, this strategy is developed by guestimating how much money you will need at retirement and then calculating how much money you will need to fund your annuity to reach that amount.

There are many pay-out options available when you decide to receive your funds, including:

- ***Straight Life Income Option***—gives you a guaranteed income for your lifetime. If this option is selected and you die before the funds are depleted, the balance of the fund is collected by the insurance company and used to help pay those who have lived beyond where the income they have or will receive is greater than their annuity. This option generally pays the most income per month than other payout options.

- *Cash Refund Option*—provides for a guaranteed income for life. However, if you die before the funds are depleted, a lump sum payment for any balance remaining in the annuity is distributed to your named beneficiaries.

- *Installment Refund Option*—similar to the cash refund option. The installment refund option guarantees that the total amount of the annuity will either be paid-out to you or, if you die before the account is depleted, to your beneficiaries. The difference between the cash refund option and the installment option is that the payment to the beneficiaries, if any, will be in installments rather than a lump sum cash payment.

- *Life With Period Certain*—designed to pay you for life and guarantees a minimum period of payments. If you die before the minimum period the beneficiaries receive the balance of the annuity contract. On the other hand, if you outlive the 'period certain', the beneficiaries would receive nothing.

- *Period Certain Option*—guarantees payments for a fixed period of time and at the end of the specified time, the payments cease whether or not you are living. Obviously, the risk here is outliving the annuity. However, period certain options can also play a very useful roll in 'laddering' several policies which begin and end at different times.

- *Joint and Full Survivor Option*—designed for a couple and provides payments through the life of the last to die. When the last survivor dies the payments cease. This can be established for full payment to continue after the first person dies or the payments can be reduced for the surviving annuitant.

It is critically important that the insurance company be of extremely sound financial strength since that will determine whether the annuity will be there when you need it. Indeed, many insurance experts will say that the financial strength of the insurance company is the single most important factor in considering any annuity product.

Your greatest safety will, of course, be with insurance carriers rated at least "AA" or preferably "AAA". While lower rated carriers, such as "B" rated carriers, usually offer higher rates of return (which is necessary for them to attract customers), you will have to do some soul-searching to determine whether a slightly higher payout is worth the risk. The truth is that insurance companies only very rarely fail and even when they do fail they almost always have huge reserves that make their policyholder whole or at least close to it. On top of that, most states keep designated funds set aside in case of an insurance company failure. Yet, who really wants to risk their retirement funds being held up for months or even years while the insurance company's assets are being liquidated?

You can verify the status of insurance companies by contacting your state department of insurance. You can go to the National Association of Insurance Commissioners web site to find your state's insurance department contact information. Go to www.naic.org and click on the USA map to find your state's information.

To spread this risk, it is suggested that you may be better off purchasing a couple of annuities from different insurance companies than a single large annuity from only one company. While the downside to this strategy may be that you might miss certain discount breakpoints for purchasing a single large annuity from one company, you have greatly reduced your risk of loss of the one company failing.

As you can see, the purchase of annuities is complex and requires the analysis of many issues and the development of a far-looking strategy that fits your particular needs. That is why it is so critically important to have a good advisor to let you know what your options are, what the hidden ins-and-outs of the policies are, and help you devise the best long-term strategy for you.

9

Fixed and Single Premium Annuities

If the rate-of-return of an annuity is a set interest percentage and not tied to the market, it is known as a Fixed Annuity. An annuity funded with a one-time single payment is known as a Single Premium Annuity.

Fixed Annuity

The simplest form of an annuity is the Fixed Annuity. It is safe, earnings are tax-deferred until the money is withdrawn, interest is compounded and there are no up-front costs or fees. Fixed annuities usually pay a higher interest rate than other fixed income instruments and because they are tax deferred you don't have to deal with those messy 1099s each year.

Generally, the Fixed Annuity is credited with either the current rate, which is defined each year by the insurer based on their investment success, or some guaranteed minimum interest rate, whichever is larger. The amount credited to your account is guaranteed to be no less than the minimum rate. With a Fixed Annuity, you know that your return will be no less than x % and nothing can change it. It is investment certainty at its finest.

The interest rate is largely a function of what the insurance company's competitors are offering and what competing investments of equivalent investment safety are offering, such as bonds. Although Fixed Annuities offer the tremendous advantage of tax-deferred growth, they still must stay competitive with these other products. Usually, the rate paid by Fixed Annuities does not have the hidden Alternative Minimum Tax (AMT) trap that sometimes ensnares municipal bond holders.

Fixed annuities can satisfy your "income you can't outlive" needs. Their payment options are pretty much the same options available to all annuities as discussed earlier. This means that in evaluating a Fixed Annuity you are left with the issue of interest rates, financial stability of the insurance company and whether you will need any money from the annuity during the period when surrender charges are applicable. Although Fixed Annuities seem relatively simple, like any other financial product they require a good long-term strategy to make them most effective.

The obvious downside to a Fixed Annuity is that the interest rate will be relatively low and may or may not keep pace with inflation. Since the purpose of an annuity is to provide retirement income until death, the threat of not keeping up with inflation can be a significant issue.

In accounts receivable financing, Fixed Annuities are rarely used because their interest rate is at risk of being exceeded by the adjustable interest due to the lender. This is why Equity Indexed Annuities (discussed later) are the more popular alternative for A/R financing programs.

Single Premium Annuities

Many accounts receivable financing programs use annuities that have only a single premium, since this allows for the entire loan to be taken against the A/R at once—thus, providing for immediate asset protection of the A/R. Single Premium Annuities are also used if you are converting to an annuity from some other product or plan, such as rolling over your 401(k) or IRA, etc.

As discussed previously, annuities can be Deferred Annuities where payments will start later or they can begin to make annuity payments to you right after purchase (Immediate Annuities). When an Immediate Annuity is purchased all at once with only one single premium payment, it is perhaps not surprisingly referred to as a Single Premium Immediate Annuity (or "SPIA"—pronounced "spee-uh").

Some advantages of SPIAs are:

- Immediate Annuities often will pay a higher rate of interest than other fixed interest instruments;

- The annuity allows you to begin or continue postponing taxes on gains that you may have received in other financial products until you actually receive your annuity payments;

- Your payments are guaranteed by the assets of the insurance company; and,

- Many states' laws exempt annuities from creditor attachment, though no similar protection is offered to other fixed income instruments.

With a SPIA you may select a period certain, a one-life only, or a joint-and-last-survivor payment schedule. It is specifically designed to provide a stream of income for a period of time that is dependent on the amount of the annuity and the expected life span of the annuitant, or the annuitants in the case of a joint-and-last-survivor annuity.

SPIAs are, frankly, almost never used in accounts receivable financing because there is no tax-deferred interest compounding with a SPIA. Instead, most annuities in accounts receivable financing involve a Single Premium Annuity that has a deferred annuitization date, known as Single Premium Deferred Annuity (SPDA).

As an aside, SPDAs are also popularly used to convert an IRA or a 401(k) type fund to satisfy, if applicable, the Required Minimum Distribution requirements of the IRS when distribution of the funds is not yet desired.

With sufficient cash, sometimes it is a good idea to purchase more than one annuity to 'ladder' the withdrawals so that not all the money starts coming out at the same time. Good financial planning will anticipate when money is needed and to defer payments as long as possible for maximum growth.

For example, you can have an SPIA begin immediate payments for the first 10-year period from one insurance company and then a SPDA to begin in 10 years for the second 10-year period, etc. This may be especially applicable to joint-and-last-survivor programs where the total funds are not needed immediately. Buying multiple annuities also provides a greater measure of security by diversifying insurance companies and diversifying investment options.

A Single Premium Immediate Annuity is not considered a good application for A/R financing because you need to maintain the tax-deferred benefit and to compound the interest over a longer period. Conversely, the Single Premium Deferred Annuity (usually in the form of an Equity Indexed Annuity, which is described in the next chapter) is the most often used type of annuity in accounts receivable financing.

10

Equity Indexed Annuities (EIA)

The Fixed Annuity is good because you are guaranteed to get at least your principal investment back but is also bad because the rate of return on your investment will be low. In the context of accounts receivable financing, this creates the realistic possibility of your arbitrage going in reverse, i.e., ending up with less money than if you had never done the A/R financing to begin with. Plainly, this is unsuitable.

We are not going to spend time discussing Variable Annuities, which as their name suggests vary with the stock markets—down as well as up—because the risk of loss of principal is too great, their internal fees and expenses make them unsuitable for the arbitrage against the loan that is needed to make accounts receivable financing work from an economic point of view, and Rule 11(d)(1) of the Securities Act of 1934 presents difficult technical hurdles to the implementation of the debt financing of Variable Annuities.

The annuity product that is most typically used in accounts receivable is the Equity Indexed Annuity (EIA), which is sometimes referred to as an Equity Indexed Linked Annuity.

An Equity Indexed Annuity is a fixed annuity that pays a baseline return, but which has a linking feature that will pay you some figure based on the performance of a market index, *whichever has yielded the higher return at the end of the term.* However, some policies may provide an interim balance that you can access for cash based on the value of the market index participation to date.

Because EIAs provide the safety and guaranteed minimum return of a fixed annuity yet also offer the chance for some market index participation, they have become the most popular of all annuity products and their sales have grown tremendously in the last several years.

Basic Concept

Perhaps the best way to think of an EIA is that it is a Fixed Annuity with an index-linked kicker. An EIA has two ways to grow, a guaranteed minimum payout based on an interest rate specified by the insurance company and a maximum payout that is tied through a complex formula to a stock market index, mostly commonly the S&P 500. At the end of the EIA's term, you would automatically get the higher value of either the fixed interest rate calculation or the formula calculation based on the performance of the stock market index.

Thus, if the stock market takes off, your EIA would have a chance to participate in the gains of the stock market index to a significant degree. But if the stock market goes sour and stays down during the period that you hold your EIA, then you would get at least the guaranteed fixed interest rate. To a very significant degree, EIAs offer a "Heads You Win, Tails You Don't Lose" opportunity to investors, which accounts for their tremendous popularity.

But of course, there is no free lunch in the financial markets, and EIAs also have their downsides. The fixed interest rate offered by EIAs will often be lower than traditional Fixed Annuities. Similarly, the formula that is used to link the EIA to the stock market index will almost never give a full participation in the index, but instead will limit it to some portion based either on percentages, so-called "caps" that limit the upside during certain periods, and other often complex restrictions.

There are many different EIA products available and many different ways that particular EIAs measure their value against movements in the stock market indices. Which method of measuring works best can only be determined by hindsight, since different methods will perform better or worse than others depending on how and/or when the market goes up and down. Suffice it to say that you are likely to get a better overall return by having several smaller EIAs with different methods for calculating their value, rather than have one large EIA with a single method. If your advisor does not advise you to do this, then you need another advisor.

As the most commonly used EIA index, the S&P-500 represents a broad cross-section of common stocks traded on the New York Stock Exchange, the American Stock Exchange and NASDAQ. This index is a selection of 500 leading companies from 100 distinct industry groups found in 10 leading industry sectors. These sectors include energy, industrials, health care, utilities, communication services, etc.

A benchmark for the performance of the index is established at the time you establish the EIA and the movement (increases or decreases) from that benchmark is documented and reported in certain intervals, which may be monthly or annually, etc. If the sum of the group, for example, moves up two points above the benchmark, the index value will rise by 2 points above the last reported interval. Similarly, if the performance of the group declines by 4 points during the next measurement point, the index will report a 4 point decline from the previous report.

If the stock market performs well, the annuity will receive good returns. However, if the market turns bearish and performs poorly, the annuity contract guarantees that at the end of the term the account will be paid the minimum interest rate rather than take a loss. How can you beat that?

For more information about indexes, see www.nasdaq.com and www.spglobal.com.

Since EIAs are usually considered to be Fixed Annuities, they are not currently considered to be a security. However, the complexity of these products has attracted the attention of the NASD and the state securities regulators, who may soon begin imposing suitability requirements on the sale of these products. An Investor Alert issued by the NASD is included in Appendix "C", *Equity-Indexed Annuities: A Complex Choice.*

Participation Rate and Indexing Methods

The funds in an equity annuity are not invested directly into a stock market fund or a mutual fund. You do not own shares in a fund as in the variable annuity products. In fact, depending on the company, their particular product and other factors, you may be offered only a percentage of the total index's gain. This is called the "participation rate" and generally is one of the factors that distinguish various plans between competitive companies. Participation rates range anywhere from 55 % to 100% depending on the indexing method and the company.

You will also be asked to select an indexing method. Although there are a number of these, the most popular methods are averaging, point-to-point, high-water mark and annual reset.

Averaging

Averaging looks back at a series of points during the index period (i.e. daily, monthly, quarterly, etc) and determines an average for the period. If the average of the actual measurements for the period is greater than the index at the start of the period, then an index average number is determined, converted into a percentage and credited to the account. Normally, the averaging method provides a 100 % participation rate; however, there may be a cap on the percentage of increase. If the number is a negative number at the end of the term, the guaranteed minimum interest rate is applied.

Averaging is a good method because it eliminates the unfortunate situation where the start point was high and the low-point just happened to occur on the anniversary date but there were great gains in the middle. Although the highest rate may not be obtained, the potential for a very low rate is also substantially reduced.

Point-to-Point

The point-to-point method divides the index on the anniversary date by the index on the previous anniversary date and subtracts 1 from the result. This method ignores all the fluctuations in between which makes the method the easiest to understand and to calculate. If the index value on the last day of a term is greater than the index value at the start of the term, an index benefit credit is calculated and credited to the annuitant's account. Participation rates may vary dramatically between companies and have been as low as 55%. Normally, a cap is also used to limit the upside of the gain for the period.

The downside of the method is that the timing of the point measurement may not be when the markets are performing at their peak and any swings during the interim period are not factored into the final growth.

High-Water Mark

The high-water mark method looks at various points during the period, and then credits the interest to the annuitant's account based on the difference between the highest indexed value during the index period as measured against the beginning index. For example, if the measurement period is from June to June and the highest point occurred in the month of September during that June to June year, the amount credited to the annuitant's account would be the amount of increase reflected in the September point.

Annual Reset

This method is similar to the point-to point (i.e. looks at the end of each contract anniversary date and locks in the gain). The difference between the two is that each time the new index point is established it becomes the new ground zero.

Any gains are locked in. Because of the nature of this method, participation rates and the caps may be set low as compared to other methods.

As an example, let's assume you chose the S & P-500 index and at the time it was at 1,200 points and you had $10,000 in the annuity. The next year the index increased to 1,320 points, a 10% increase which is credited to your account and the value of the account became $11,000. The second year the index drops to 900. The new ground zero then becomes 900 and you don't have to wait until the index gets back to 1,320 points to regain your potential gains. Your gains have thus been locked in, and the index value has been reset at the end of each year. You will begin receiving new gains when the index moves above 900 or resets itself.

You can expect this method would have a low participation rate and a fairly low cap to limit the amount of interest you may earn each year.

So Which Method Is Best?

It depends how the stock market performs, which is to say that you will only know with hindsight which method was the best. Because of this, good planners will not stuff all your money into a single crediting method, but will instead spread your money around several crediting methods (and several products if necessary) to give you the best chance of overall performance. Beware the agent who would take all of your money and put it into a single EIA with a single crediting method, for that advisor may not be looking out for your best interests. At the same time, you may run across lenders who will not allow you to put all your money into more than one product because they desire only single collateral.

Keep in mind that when considering an EIA you should plan for the minimum guaranteed interest, and take any gains above that as gravy. The market is going to fluctuate up and down but should be positive in the long term. As with most other successful financial strategies, intelligent diversification is often the key to success.

Beware the Surrender Charges!

For accounts receivable financing, the downside to an EIA is that many products have lengthy surrender charges. The obvious problem that this creates is that if the lender calls your accounts receivable loan and collects against your EIA, you may get stuck paying the surrender charges. Most accounts receivable financing arrangements will allow the lender to proceed first against the annuity or life insurance that is placed as additional security, which of course they will do instead of sitting around waiting for checks to come into the business. The lender could frankly care less about the surrender charges since it will be you that makes up the difference.

Indeed, an insurance agent who puts the funds from an accounts receivable financing arrangement into an EIA with substantial and long-term surrender charges may be doing you a great disservice—unless you will have other funds available to pay off the loan if need be. Because of this, many of the turnkey accounts receivable financing arrangements utilize EIAs that either have no surrender charges, or the surrender charges will be waived if the loan is called during the surrender period.

The flip side to all this is, however, that some of these EIA products may not be the most competitive with others on the market. Those with the longer surrender periods will often perform better than those without because the insurance company can anticipate that more purchasers will stay in their programs over the long-term, and thus they can take a longer and more efficient view of how they should themselves invest.

The key, as always, is having a good advisor who is familiar with these programs that get you into products that make sense for your situation. A good advisor will have several illustrations from various companies on various products for you to compare and see for yourself the strengths and weaknesses of each product in your particular case.

PART III
Life Insurance

Because of its potential for tax-deferred growth and uses for estate and business planning, life insurance is a popular alternative for many accounts receivable financing programs. Here, we explore life insurance and several of its most common variants.

Chapter 11—Introduction to Life Insurance—A discussion of what life insurance is, how most policies operate, asset protection features, and tax and insurable interest considerations.

Chapter 12—Term Life Insurance—Temporary life insurance that is rarely used in accounts receivable financing because no cash value is built up to be available as collateral.

Chapter 13—Whole Life Insurance—Permanent life insurance which builds cash value that can be loaned to you, but is also a very inflexible product.

Chapter 14—Universal Life Insurance—Much greater flexibility and the ability to make withdrawals against the cash value, so long as it is not a Modified Endowment Contract (MEC).

Chapter 15—Equity Indexed Life Insurance—The life insurance equivalent of Equity Indexed Annuities, this product offers a minimum guaranteed return with the chance for higher growth through market participation.

Note that we will not be covering Variable Life or Variable Universal Life ("VUL") insurance, because they suffer from many of the same difficulties as Variable Annuities for use in accounts receivable financing programs (i.e., the variable nature is too risky for lenders to accept as collateral); there is a potential Rule 11(d)(1) problem; and, other concerns.

11

Introduction to Life Insurance

You can love it or hate it, but you will have to admit that the tax-deferred build-up of cash value within a life insurance policy makes it an extremely useful financial planning tool. Because a significant purpose of accounts receivable financing is to attempt to take advantage of opportunities for tax-deferred growth and tax-free distribution, the use of life insurance (which offers both) as a receptacle for the loan proceeds must be explored.

It's all about death and taxes. Death is, indeed, certain. Life insurance is really "death insurance" though it cannot protect you from death (having it known as "life insurance" must rate as one of the greatest marketing accomplishments of all time). But, in the event of death, a life insurance policy can provide for the beneficiaries and perhaps even provide some extra money to take care of that other certainty—taxes.

Some of the most important benefits of life insurance relate to how it is treated for income tax purposes when properly structured:

- earnings accumulated within policies with cash value grow tax-deferred;

- you can borrow against the cash value during your lifetime on a tax-free basis, with the option of repaying your loan at death from the policy's death benefits; and,

- death benefits are paid to your beneficiaries free of any income or capital gains taxes (and, potentially, estate taxes if the life insurance is purchased outside of your estate).

While life insurance is used primarily to protect against an early death, certain types of life insurance can also be used to provide retirement income. From a family protection perspective, this is where most insurance policies are directed. They provide enormous benefits to your family if you die too soon, but also provide a retirement savings account for you.

With some life insurance products you can accumulate a significant amount of value within the policy. This value can be accessed by you through a low-interest loan so that when you pass away, the remaining value goes to your beneficiaries free of any income taxes as part of the policy's death benefit. You can also access the cash value by surrendering the policy back to the insurance company, or sometimes even selling the policy to an investor in what is known as a Life Settlement.

Other uses for life insurance extend far beyond financial protection for dependents in the event of your death. It is also an important product in maintaining the continuity of businesses, in estate planning, in retirement planning and, in many ways, wealth management and asset protection programs. Some variants of life insurance allow you to participate in the movements of the stock market to grow cash value. You can use life insurance to insure your home mortgage. You can even use it to entice key personnel to stay with your company. Life insurance has so many uses in today's society and business world it is difficult to enumerate all of the possibilities.

But life insurance policies can be very complicated. In addition to the standard disclaimers and contractual conditions, life insurance policies have a number of riders and options available that deal with specific issues and administrative preferences. Those issues are outside the scope of this book but should be thoroughly understood and evaluated prior to entering into a life insurance contract.

Asset Protection

Life insurance can be a powerful asset protection tool, for the reason that the laws of many states specifically exempt life insurance policies from the collection efforts of creditors. But this protection is spotty and whether creditors can get at the cash value in your life insurance policy may depend on which side of a state line you are on and what the terms provide. In developing your accounts receivable financing strategy, it is critical that you work with an attorney who is familiar with your state exemptions for life insurance, annuities, and other products, so they can guide you as to which product affords the greatest asset protection.

If you do not live in a state that protects life insurance and annuities, then it is imperative that you invest the proceeds from your accounts receivable financing into an asset protected structure and have it purchase the life insurance policy. The beneficiary-taxed irrevocable trust, or "BETIR trust", which is discussed in Chapter 4 is ideal for this purpose. You should consult with an attorney who practices in the area of asset protection planning to make sure that however your life insurance policy is held, it will have a good chance of being protected from creditors.

Even in those states that protect life insurance and annuities from creditors, you should also consider asset protection for the life insurance policy. There are several reasons for this, including that the state exemptions do not protect against things like federal tax liability. Also, a smart creditor might try to find a way to get at your life insurance policy by attempting to collect against your policy in a state that does not protect such products (such as where the insurance company is located). While years down the road you might or might not win on the issue of which state's laws apply, in the interim your investment might be tied up at a time when you really need it.

Moreover, by placing your life insurance into an asset protection structure, you also may help your heirs get a start on their asset protection by shielding the proceeds from their creditors, ex-spouses, and the like.

Thus, no matter what type of insurance or financial product you use to invest the proceeds from your accounts receivable financing, you must consider holding your investment in a trust that has creditor protections for beneficiaries. The reason is simple: If you and your spouse suddenly die, your investments will pass to your children. If they pass directly to your children, they become potentially exposed to your children's creditors and spouses. By using the assets to fund a properly-drafted spendthrift trust—even if you control it during your lifetime—you have done your children a great favor by helping with their asset protection as well.

Again, the key is to have a top-notch asset protection attorney design or at least review your arrangement to make sure that it is sound.

Beneficiaries

The beneficiary is the person (or entity) legally entitled to receive the death benefit proceeds of the life insurance policy in the event you die while the policy is in effect. A beneficiary can be a revocable beneficiary, meaning you can change the beneficiary at any time without the beneficiary's consent, or it can be an irrevocable beneficiary, meaning the beneficiary's interest in the policy cannot be changed without his or her consent. The irrevocable beneficiary effectively becomes a co-owner of the policy and his or her consent must be obtained in all policy transactions.

You can and should name more than one beneficiary. You can name a primary beneficiary and one or more secondary (contingent) beneficiaries or even a third level (tertiary) beneficiary in the event the primary and secondary beneficiaries are deceased at the time of your death. Without a named beneficiary, state law will dictate where the proceeds will go and it may not be where you would have wished them to go.

Estates may also be named as the beneficiary—although doing so is not recommended. Life insurance proceeds that go to estates increase the size of the estate thus simultaneously increasing any state or federal estate tax. It may also trigger a time consuming probate or become vulnerable to the attack of your creditors (who become your estate's creditors). Life insurance should instead be owned by heirs or within an Irrevocable Life Insurance Trust (ILIT) when possible so that the IRS will consider the life insurance proceeds to be paid outside the estate for purposes of estate taxes.

Accessing the Cash Value

The rights of policyholders to access the cash value are pretty standard in all life insurance policies, but they are an especially important consideration for accounts receivable financing.

There are five basic types of life insurance policies and four of those policy types develop a cash value within the policy which you are allowed to access. Term Life insurance does not accumulate a cash value and, therefore, there is nothing to access. A Whole Life policy allows you to borrow against the accumulated cash value and its cousins, Universal Life and Variable Life policies, allow you to withdraw a portion of the cash value.

A Whole Life policy has a provision that outlines how you may borrow from the policy. Policy loans are not considered distributions. If you have borrowed against your policy and then die before repaying the loan, the insurance company would use the death proceeds to pay off the loan. Thus, your beneficiary would receive the face value of the policy less the amount that was loaned to you and any interest accrued while the loan was outstanding.

When you borrow from the cash value of your life insurance policy, you will be assessed an interest fee until the funds are repaid. There is no contractual requirement for you to repay the loan during your lifetime; however, by not repaying the loan the interest will continue to accrue. Unless new funds are paid into the policy, the loan interest will eventually eat away all the cash value and the policy will lapse. Moreover, the interest you pay on the loan is not deductible for your income tax purposes.

You can also withdraw the cash value in its entirety and surrender a Whole Life policy back to the insurance company. Think of it as you reselling your policy back to the company at a price determined by whatever is left in it. In that event, the amount of funds that exceed the cost basis (i.e., your investment gains within the policy) will be taxed to you as ordinary income.

It can sometimes make more sense to convert the cash value of a life insurance policy to an annuity, which should be a tax-free "1035 exchange" if done correctly. Converting the life insurance to an annuity allows you access to the funds and to continue the tax-deferral benefits until withdrawn (for retirement purposes, for example).

In the Universal Life and Variable Life products a schedule is often provided that restricts your ability to withdraw funds from your account. These restrictions are known as "surrender charges". In the early years the penalty for withdrawal may be quite high, but it is generally reduced each year until the 12th or possibly up to the 15th year, and thereafter there is no penalty. Withdrawal of funds, however, will reduce the death benefit and may adversely impact the crediting of annual interest payments to the account. You can also withdraw the funds from a Universal Life and a Variable Life product and convert the cash value to an annuity under the 1035 exchange rules with no tax penalty.

The ability to access the cash value of the policy and to make a tax-free transfer to an annuity are important components of a sound accounts receivable financing plan. These are significant benefits which, if used properly and in conjunction with other planning options, can result in outstanding programs to assist your retirement and estate planning issues.

Taxes

Because of powerful lobbying by the insurance companies, Congress has given very favorable tax treatment to life insurance. The most obvious benefits are that the earnings within the life insurance contract are tax-deferred until withdrawn and that the heirs receive the death benefit free of any income or capital gains taxes. This tax-deferred treatment of life insurance policies makes them prime candidates for use with an account receivables financial plan that is designed to fund retirement or estate planning needs.

The premiums paid for life insurance policies are generally considered to be personal expenses, and thus are not deductible. However, premiums paid by employers for the benefit of their employees can be deducted by the employer as business expenses. Further, the premiums paid to fund a life insurance policy which is payable to a charity may be deductible as charitable contributions. Premiums paid under an alimony agreement may also be deductible.

The death benefits from a life insurance policy are usually exempt from federal income tax. By contrast, with an annuity the only exempt portion of any death benefit (if there is a death benefit) is the face value of the policy and the excess is taxable to the beneficiary.

Certain death benefits can also be taxed. For example, life insurance benefits received under a qualified pension or profit-sharing plan can generate income tax when they are distributed to an employee. Additionally, policy proceeds seized by a creditor, received as compensation by an employer or business owner, received as dividends from a corporation, or received as alimony, can also be taxed.

Insurable Interest

A life insurance policy must have an Insurable Interest. This means that whoever is acquiring the contract (the Applicant) must be subject to a loss on the death, illness or disability of the person being insured. Each individual has an unlimited insurable interest in his or her own life. Parents, spouses, children, brother, etc. have insurable interests in each other because of blood or marriage. A creditor-debtor relationship gives rise to an insurable interest as does a business relationship. The insurable interest must exist when the life insurance policy is written, and not necessarily at the time of the loss.

Summary

While the concept of life insurance is simple enough, the policies themselves are sometimes very complex. A discussion on risk/mortality methodology, legal terms and conditions, riders, and the structure of the industry is beyond the scope of this book. However, you have been provided with a summary of some of the important issues, such as designating a beneficiary, borrowing from the cash value, and taxes. The next few chapters will identify the types of life insurance arrangements available and provide a short discussion of their advantages and disadvantages as an accounts receivable financing tool.

For more information about life insurance you should visit the website of your state's insurance commission as well as the website of the National Association of Insurance Commissioners (NAIC) at www.naic.org. An NAIC Consumer Alert, *Tips for Buying Line Insurance*, is included in Appendix "A".

12

Term Life Insurance

Term Life insurance is the least complex and the least expensive form of life insurance. It is sometimes referred to as "temporary" insurance because it provides insurance protection only for a certain period of time. If you die after the period expires, there will be no coverage. Term Life is thus considered "pure insurance" because the only benefit is the payment of the face amount of the policy to the beneficiaries of the deceased insured. Very simply, in return for your premium payments, the insurance company promises to pay a benefit only if you die during the policy coverage period.

Term Life insurance is not used for retirement purposes. Unlike the other types of life insurance, a Term Life insurance policy does not accumulate cash value and thus there is nothing for you to borrow against if you later need cash.

During your younger years, term insurance will be cheap, meaning that an enormous amount of insurance can be obtained for a very small premium payment. As you grow older and your risk of death in a given year statistically increases, your premium will begin to rapidly increase. By that time, hopefully, your beneficiaries will not need the death benefit as much (e.g., your children will have grown up). Since there is no residual value in the policy, at some point the insurance becomes too expensive for what it might pay and so most people terminate the policy.

For a higher premium, you can purchase an option to renew a level term policy beyond the specified period. This is known as Renewable Term. This can be important because you will not have to provide evidence of insurability even if you become uninsurable for some reason. In other words, you will still be able to buy Renewable Term insurance even if you are diagnosed with a heart condition or other serious disease.

You can also purchase an option to covert the Term policy to a Whole Life policy which may also provide the guarantee to renew the policy without providing evidence of insurability if you become insurable. This is known as Convertible Term.

Term Life insurance has many uses in both your personal life and for your business. The obvious use for Term Life insurance is as financial security for your family in the event of your premature death. But Term Life insurance can also be used by small businesses, partnerships and corporations as a means of insuring the continuation of the business if the owner, partner or major shareholder should suddenly die. This is known as Buy-Sell insurance, since it funds the company's buyout of the deceased owner's interest from his or her estate.

Similarly, Term Life insurance can also be used to insure against the loss of a key employee, or for the benefit of a key's employees family as an inducement to keep the key employee on board. This is known as Key Man insurance.

Sometimes Term Life insurance is used by wealthy people as a hedge against estate taxes, mostly to limit their estate tax exposure while they are waiting for other planning to take effect. For instance, if you thought the estate tax would be fully repealed in 2010, it might make sense to purchase renewable term insurance through 2010 to hedge against estate taxes during those years when it would still apply.

As in all insurance products, there are different plans available that are designed to meet the specific needs of the insured. Term Life insurance is no exception and the industry has developed three basic policies from which to select: Level Term, Decreasing Term and Increasing Term.

The Level Term policy provides both level death benefit and level premium payments for the duration of the policy. With Level Term, the insurance company must determine the mortality rates over the complete term of the policy and spread the premium payments over the period. Thus, you would have to pay a much higher rate in the early years than the actual risk calls for in return for lower rates in the later years when the mortality risks are higher. This might not make much sense, because the real-world value of the death benefit would grow smaller and smaller because of inflation. Consequently, most Level Term policies are for a relatively short term with periodic renewal intervals to allow both parties to renegotiate the policy.

In the Decreasing Term policy the amount of death benefit protection will decrease over the term of the contract; however, your premium payments will remain level over a period which is less than the policy term. This is often used as Credit Life insurance to cover a debt, such as a home mortgage where as the debt is paid down the value of the insurance decreases.

The amount of insurance in an Increasing Term plan will increase at periodic intervals over the term of the contract in accordance with some established indices or by some prescribed amount. This type of insurance has value for a young person who may not be able to currently afford the amount of coverage they anticipate they will need in future years. The primary reason for purchasing the policy is the face amount can be increased without the insured having to provide evidence of insurability. Even if you become disabled, the insurance would still be increased as long as the premium payments are made as scheduled.

Term Life and Accounts Receivable Financing

Term Life is rarely used in accounts receivable financing for the simple reason that it has no cash value and, thus, nothing for the lender to take as collateral. However, some complex arrangements involve a strategy of taking a loan against the A/R, which is secured by other business collateral and then using the proceeds to fund a Term Life policy. This allows the business to utilize the strategy even though it lacks current liquidity. Again, these strategies will be relatively rare.

We will now explore the "permanent" life insurance solutions, beginning with Whole Life.

13

Whole Life Insurance

A Whole Life insurance policy gives protection from the date of issue to the date of your death. It covers your whole life and not just a few years. Consequently, it is often referred to as "permanent" insurance. The reason for this is very simple: whereas a Term Life insurance policy provides a death benefit only so long as you make premium payments each and every year, a fully funded Whole Life policy will provide the face amount of life insurance no matter how many years pass before you die.

In addition to providing a whole life death benefit, Whole Life also adds a new component where you can build-up cash value within the policy to fund your retirement or other needs.

Like all life insurance products that have cash value, the real advantage is the tax-deferred growth of your money within the policy as given by your good friends in Congress.

Your premium payments will create cash value within a Whole Life policy. Cash value is the sum of the premiums paid (the "cost basis"), plus interest, and less the mortality expense (the pure cost of providing death insurance during a given period) and the insurance company's expenses for maintaining the arrangement.

The interest will be paid by the insurance company in accordance with the insurance policy's stated rate. Since the company is making a long-term guaranteed interest rate, it must be conservative in its commitments and the interest rate will be relatively low. This interest will be applied to the account balance annually and compounded from year-to-year.

The formula for Whole Life cash value is:

$$Cash\ Value = (P + I) - (M + E)$$
$$P = \text{Premium Paid}$$
$$I = \text{Interest Earned}$$
$$M = \text{Mortality Expense}$$
$$E = \text{Administrative Expenses}$$

A true Whole Life insurance policy is designed to mature ("endow") when you reach the age of 100. If you pay every premium from the date of the policy issue until you attain the age of 100, the policy will be fully paid and your premium payments would cease. The cash value would be equal to the face value of the policy at that point.

A variant of Whole Life is known as Limited Pay Whole Life insurance. This policy essentially limits the payments to a specified number of years. The face value stays the same and the insurance protection extends until death or the policy endows. However, the premiums are paid for a specific period to fully pay the policy. The payment can be for a number of years (10, 20, 30, etc.) or until the insured reaches a specific age (e.g., the 65th birthday). The annual premium amount is larger for limited pay policies because the insurance company still has the obligation to continue the death benefits until you reach the age of 100. As far as the death benefit component is concerned, you are basically prepaying the benefit.

When you reach the specified date or number of years, you could either borrow against the policy to fund your retirement or it might make sense for you to exchange your policy for an annuity. If you borrow from the policy the loan does not have to be repaid. However, upon your death, the loan, along with any interest due on the loan, will be subtracted from the death benefit to be paid to your beneficiaries.

You still must keep enough cash value in the policy to pay the mortality and other expenses charged by the insurance company, or the policy will lapse. If the policy lapses or you voluntarily surrender it, any outstanding loan above the amount of premiums you paid-in could be considered a gain and taxed as ordinary income. Thus, care must be taken not to over-borrow from the policy and to leave enough cash value in the policy to sustain the policy until your death.

Since a Whole Life policy has current value even before you die, it can be used as collateral for loans, including for accounts receivable financing. The problem with Whole Life is that the interest paid by the insurance company may be low and the arbitrage against the interest on the loan and the A/R might not work out in the long-term.

Where an insurance policy has cash value, one must be careful to protect the policy from creditors. Some states exempt the cash value of life insurance policies from attachment by creditors, but many do not. In either event, it is prudent to have an asset protected structure own the life insurance policy.

Another problem with Whole Life is that it is somewhat inflexible. In the next chapter, we will examine a similar form of insurance that is not as restrictive.

14

Universal Life Insurance

We have just discussed Whole Life insurance, which is very predictable insofar that it has fixed premiums, a fixed interest rate to generate cash value and a permanent face value. You cannot vary the premiums and you cannot adjust the death benefit. A Whole Life policy is inflexible on those issues and cannot be adapted to changing circumstances. Over a long period of time, changing conditions and circumstances are likely, if not inevitable.

In this regard, Universal Life (commonly referred as "UL") insurance is just the opposite of Whole Life insurance. Importantly, UL allows for modifications for changing circumstances without having to exchange policies. With a Universal Life policy, you can vary the amount and frequency of your premium payments as your situation changes. This up-front flexibility also allows you to increase or decrease the death benefit of your policy to meet your changing needs.

Like a Term Life policy, a Universal Life policy has both the mortality component and the expense component included in the cost of insurance. And, like the Whole Life policy, the Universal Life policy also has the additional component for cash value accumulation. As premiums are paid into the policy, the mortality and expense components are deducted and the cash value component is added to the policy. The interest paid-in by the insurance company may be a guaranteed rate, a current rate which is established annually by the insurance company based on their investment successes, or a combination of the higher of a minimum guaranteed interest rate and the annually established rate.

As long as there is sufficient cash value in the policy for the insurance company to withdraw the mortality and expense components, the policy will stay in force. If the cash value does not support the monthly mortality and expense components, the policy will terminate.

Periodically, the policyowner can increase or decrease the face amount without changing the premium payments as long as there is sufficient cash value in the policy to cover the mortality and expense costs. Additionally, funds can be added to the cash value account. However, care must be taken to avoid becoming a Modified Endowment Contract ("MEC") and losing certain tax advantages unique to life insurance policies.

MECs v. non-MECs

You may hear the terms MEC and non-MEC used several times throughout discussions with program administrators, insurance agents, etc. during your search for a program that fits your needs. A MEC results from a 1988 Act that was designed to discourage the sale and purchase of life insurance for investment purposes or as a tax shelter. A MEC is treated much less favorably than a non-MEC for most tax purposes. With a non-MEC, life insurance is granted tax-deferred cash value accumulation within the policy, withdrawals are not taxed until the withdrawal exceed the amount paid into the policy, and policy loans are not considered distributions and are not taxed unless full surrender of the policy takes place.

If an insurance policy fails to qualify as a non-MEC, and is therefore a MEC, none of these features will be available. A MEC provides that from any amount taken as a loan or a withdrawal, the gains will be taxed first as ordinary income before the return on premiums. Additionally, a 10% tax penalty is imposed if withdrawals are received prior to reaching the age of 59 ½.

Most insurance planners try to avoid MECs like the plague. Once you are in, you can't get out. To avoid MEC treatment, premiums cannot be paid in one year, but instead must be spread over several years. Additionally, a "corridor test" must be met that provides that certain levels of death benefits must be provided by the policy, depending on a number of factors. Usually, planners will spread premiums payments over at least 2 years, and often 7 years. Usually, the longer you spread the premium payments, the more efficiently the policy will perform.

It is generally up to the insurance company and agent to help see that the policy is not classified as MEC. Indeed, it can be negligence by the agent if the policy fails in some aspect and thus becomes a MEC when it was intended to be a non-MEC.

As it relates to accounts receivable financing, the problem with the MEC vs. non-MEC issue is that you probably want to finance all of your receivables now, and not have any portion exposed to creditors. This may conflict with the need to pay premiums over time so as to qualify as a non-MEC. Different programs address these issues in different ways. Suffice it to say that if you have an overall asset protection plan, it shouldn't be an issue if the loan proceeds will immediately be transferred to an asset protected structured and there held until they can be contributed into the policy.

Beware programs that advise you to slowly borrow against your accounts receivable, thus leaving a portion exposed to creditors, as these programs are obviously not well thought out.

Loans and Death Benefits

Unlike a Whole Life policy which only allows you to take a loan from the cash value of the policy, a Universal Life policy also allows you to make a partial withdrawal from the cash value as long as there are sufficient funds in the policy to support the mortality and expense components. Additionally, you may surrender the Universal Life policy for its entire cash value although there may be a surrender charge if the policy has not been in force for a number of years.

Universal Life insurance policies generally offer two death benefit options. Under Option A you can designate a specific amount of death benefit. As the cash value grows the insurance portion of the benefit decreases. However, you must be careful that the additional premiums do not cause the policy to violate the corridor test.

In Option B you designate the death benefit to be the face amount plus the cash value and in Option B the insurance component does not decrease with the cash value accumulation. Care must be taken to insure the cash value is not disproportionately larger than the term insurance portion.

Although most Universal Life insurance policies are very similar, subtle differences in interest rates, rider options and mortality expenses distinguish the various Universal Life companies from each other and these features should be compared when shopping for a Universal Life policy.

Because of the inherent flexibilities of Universal Life insurance policies they are used extensively in buy-sell agreements, key-person insurance, executive bonus arrangements, split dollar plans and, importantly, in accounts receivable financing.

15

Equity Indexed Life Insurance

Very similar to the Equity Indexed Annuity, discussed in Chapter 10, is the concept of Equity Indexed Life insurance ("EILI" or sometimes "EI Life"). This form of life insurance provides a minimum internal return based on a fixed rate, with the chance for upwards participation according to the stock market index against which it is linked. While these policies have been around in one form or another for some years, it is has not been until the boom of equity indexed annuities that they have themselves grown in popularity.

The problem with Variable Universal Life ("VUL") insurance, which we will not discuss because it is unsuitable for accounts receivable financing for the same reasons as Variable Annuities, is that if the investment return during the first several years is negative, the policy may never recuperate to be able to catch up with increasing death benefit costs. Thus, many VUL policies whose investments underperform during the first several years become at risk of failing.

By providing a minimum return, equity indexed life insurance substantially mitigates against loss during the early policy years, while giving the policy a chance for good performance if the market index swings upwards. Some EILI policies allow for later conversion to VUL policies after a period of years and the threat of early policy failure has subsided.

Equity Indexed Life insurance policies are probably ideal solutions for accounts receivable financing. These policies have many of the same tax and collateral benefits of Universal Life policies. The caveat is that sometimes their investment performance may not be sufficient to win the arbitrage against the loan interest rates. As with Universal Life policies, one must also be cautious about the period over which the policy is funded to ensure that it is treated as a non-MEC.

As Equity Indexed Annuities continue to boom, there will be more and better Equity Indexed Life Insurance products coming to the market, and thus more choices to use with accounts receivable financing. It is certainly worth reviewing competing illustrations with these products against Whole Life and Universal Life insurance policies.

PART IV
Other Considerations

In this final part of the book, we discuss the alternatives to accounts receivable financing, including structured solutions and factoring, and then give some tips on how you can find a program that is right for you.

Chapter 16—Structured Solutions—Considers privately financed arrangements and those that contribute the proceeds into ERISA programs to increase the benefits.

Chapter 17—Factoring—Discusses the predecessor to accounts receivable financing which involves selling your A/R at a discount.

Chapter 18—Finding the Right Program For You—A discussion of programs and promoters and a re-emphasis of having an attorney involved to protect your interests.

Additional Information—Information about my website at http://www.farbook.com

16

Structured Solutions

With accounts receivable financing there is no requirement that you put the proceeds of the loan into an insurance product. Most people use an insurance product vehicle because it is easy and efficient to do so. However, such a product will not fit every instance.

One big advantage to using an insurance product to hold and invest the financing proceeds is that the insurance product will always be available to pay back the loan, if necessary. Since many businessmen may not always have the day-to-day liquidity themselves to repay the loan, if for whatever reason it is called, they will essentially be limited to this sort of product.

For other businesses that have a great deal of liquidity (or their owners have a great deal of liquidity) and are capable of essentially self-financing their accounts receivables, it will sometimes make sense to use the financing proceeds to capitalize a heavily asset protected entity, such as a Limited Liability Company (LLC), and then within the LLC invest the money into the stock market or similar investments on a managed account basis. The goal here is to generate an ever higher rate of return than would have been generated within the insurance product, so that the A/R financing arbitrage becomes even more favorable to the business owner.

The reason that LLCs are usually used for this purpose is that they share, with limited partnerships, the benefits of so-called "charging order protection". This means that if a creditor of a member of the LLC comes along, the creditor will not get the assets of the LLC but will instead be limited to a "charging order" that has the effect of redirecting to the creditor those profit distributions that would have been made to the debtor. In many ways, it is like an "assignment of income" that is received from the LLC.

Thus, if the business invests in an LLC and receives membership interests in return, those membership interests will usually be very hard for a creditor of the business to get, especially if the type of membership interest by the business is in the form of a "non-managing membership interest", i.e., a passive interest. A typical arrangement would have the business as the 99% non-managing member and the business owner (or, better, a trust formed for the benefit of the business owner) as the 1% managing member. This would give the business owner direct investment control, but still protect the investment funds within the LLC from creditors of the business.

Once the financing proceeds are in the LLC they can be loaned out to fulfill whatever investment purposes the business owner desires to make (subject to the lender's lien on those funds, as discussed below). Thus, if the business owner desires to invest in a real estate project, the LLC can be either an equity investor or a lender in that project.

At some point, some or all of the interests in the LLC can be sold from the business to the owner, perhaps as a return-of-principal. This then would have the effect of transferring the wealth that is in the LLC to the business owner. The LLC interest might also be sold into a family trust by way of a private annuity agreement or self-canceling installment note (SCIN), so as to further estate planning purposes as well.

To secure the lender on the A/R financing, the proceeds will typically be held in a segregated investment account with the lender having a lien on that account. When the loan is paid off, either with the funds in the LLC or more likely by the business, the investments funds become free-and-clear.

Again, the advantage to this arrangement is investment flexibility. The downside, of course, is the additional cost of structuring and maintaining the LLC, plus the fact that investment growth within the LLC would not be tax-deferred as it would be in a life insurance product or in an annuity. But for those who believe they can invest in either a tax-efficient way or who can consistently yield such higher returns such that taxes are not a consideration, then this alternative strategy may make sense.

ERISA Plans

The Valhalla of Accounts Receivable Financing is to use the finance proceeds to fund an ERISA plan for the business. Because funding an ERISA plan is a legitimate business purpose, the interest payments on the loan should be deductible by the business. Even better than that, the business would get a current-year income tax deduction for every dollar paid in the plan. And if that weren't gravy enough, all the assets held in an ERISA-qualified trust are automatically protected from creditors under what is known as the ERISA anti-alienation provisions.

Since using the financing proceeds to fund an ERISA plan seems like the obvious solution, one must wonder why all A/R financing strategies do not do this. The problem is that ERISA plans have significant limitations, including annual limits on the amount of money that can be paid into them, and sometimes a requirement that all the employees of the business be included in the plan. There are also significant restrictions on when, how, and in what amounts moneys may be taken out of these plans. Despite the huge advantages, figuring all this out can be a lot of work, and requires the development of a detailed strategy for funding, maintaining, and then withdrawing money from the ERISA plan.

The other disadvantage to using the finance proceeds to fund an ERISA plan derives from one of the principal advantages of such plans: namely, that the funds within an ERISA plan are protected by the so-called "anti-alienation provisions" that keep them from being used as security or collateral for precisely the sort of lending arrangements that accounts receivable financing constitute. In other words, you can contribute the finance proceeds into an ERISA plan, but the lender's security interest might not be able follow them in there. There may also be serious and extremely negative tax consequences for having a leveraged asset in such a plan (some promoters attempt to contribute leveraged annuities or life insurance into a VEBA—beware!).

What this means in practice is that the business owner will have to find other liquid assets to use as collateral for the accounts receivable financing. While this can seem like a hassle, it actually creates a considerable advantage insofar as those assets would then be effectively stripped of their equity as well. Those assets would be unattractive to creditors as well so long as the loan and security agreement continues to exist.

While there is a great deal of work in making blended A/R financing and ERISA plans work together, the benefits as mentioned are enormous because of the current-year income tax deduction to the business, tax-deferred growth within the ERISA plan, sometimes tax-favorable withdrawal from the ERISA plan, and always tremendous asset protection of both the A/Rs and the finance proceeds that were contributed to the plan. It's a lot of work—and absolutely requires the participation of a tax attorney who is skilled with ERISA plans—but it can be definitely worth it, even if not all of the finance proceeds go into the ERISA plan.

If it were practicable in your situation, your advisor should have discussed the possibilities of blending your A/R financing program with an ERISA plan. If not, then you definitely need a new advisor because you potentially missed a big planning opportunity.

17

Factoring

The financing of accounts receivable is not the only game in town, and certainly not the oldest. Accounts receivable factoring, sometimes called Invoice Discounting or sometimes Invoice Financing, is an ages old financial practice that involves a business which sells its accounts receivables in order to receive immediate cash. The company that purchases the receivables by providing the advance payment is known as the "Factor".

There are many reasons to factor receivables, some of which may be:

- to obtain a source of working capital that may not be available through other sources;

- to purchase equipment or inventory on demand;

- to take advantage of vendor discounts;

- to have cash available to meet immediate management and personnel needs

- to provide extended credit to valued customers; and,

- to free yourself of the time consuming process of collecting outstanding invoices

As discussed previously, your accounts receivable represent a non-productive asset. While the receivables are outstanding your business does not have access to the monies and you cannot put those dollars to work making money for your company. Actually, A/Rs can be thought of as an interest-free loan to your company's customers. By selling the invoice to a factoring receivable company your business gains immediate access to a portion of those funds for use in the business.

Generally, a factoring company will provide cash for 70% to 90% of the outstanding receivables. The actual percentage will depend upon the credit worthiness of your clients. The factoring company assumes the receivables and the responsibility for collection. Once the receivables have been collected, you will then receive the balance of the receivables less a small fee from the factoring company. The amount of the fee charged by the factoring company, again, is negotiated based on the credit worthiness of the clients but you can expect to pay anywhere from 2% to 5% of the total receivables as the factoring company's fees. Fees vary from factoring companies and from client to client and are based on customer base, payment cycle, invoice size and, of course, credit worthiness for the business and for the businesses' clients.

The primary advantages of accounts receivable factoring are that it provides immediate cash and mitigates the need to incur debt while waiting for invoices to be paid. It also eliminates the need to spend valuable management time collecting and tracking invoices and, since the factoring companies are generally professionals who specialize in collecting payments due, the ratio of bad debts is usually improved.

The primary disadvantage, or downside, to accounts receivable factoring is that it is not cheap. The total cost may be more than the cost of a short-term commercial loan. Factoring also tends to be a one-shot deal, which means that new account receivables that the business generates will be exposed to creditors of the business.

Although the process requires some negotiation and verification, it does not require a lengthy loan approval process nor does it require using other assets for collateral. Verification may require a statement about your business, information about your customers and an accounts receivables aging report (i.e. the businesses' past collection experience). To qualify, the business must have a reputable product or service and credit-worthy customers.

Sometimes it makes sense for a business to factor its accounts receivable, instead of financing them. Since these are usually specialty situations, they are beyond the scope of this book. We have included this discussion of factoring only so that you will be able to recognize the difference in the programs.

18

Finding the Right Program for You

Your chances of getting into an accounts receivable programs that works for you are probably lower than your chances of getting into one that doesn't. The reason for this, as mentioned earlier, is that nobody is looking out for your interests or trying to make sure that the program is optimized for you. Plus, there are some poorly designed programs being marketed that you could stumble into, which will further lower your chances of getting into the right one.

If you need accounts receivable financing, then you need to be in a program that works for you. When accounts receivable financing is done poorly it can turn out to be a nightmare, but when it works properly it can be a very powerful financing tool to leverage an underutilized asset into much greater retirement savings.

Accounts receivable financing programs are relatively complex but the training that is given to the agents who sell them is often minimal and limited to teaching the agents how to fill out the forms. This will simply not do for such a complex transaction. The key to effective accounts receivable financing is finding an advisor—usually a tax or business planning attorney—who will help you to evaluate your situation and compare alternatives, optimize a program that fits your specific needs, and then review the documents the lender presents to you to make sure your needs are fully protected.

The need to hire an attorney to represent your interest in these deals cannot be emphasized enough. Otherwise, you are at the whims of a "canned" accounts receivable program that will fit you no better than a one-size-fits-all sports jacket. You will probably end-up with transactional documents that will only protect the lender's interests at your expense.

Another key to having a good accounts receivable financing program is to make sure that the most likely contingencies are addressed in advance. As related earlier, it is critically important that the financial product the loan proceeds are ultimately invested in is independently asset protected. It is not enough to simply rely on state exemptions for life insurance or annuities, since bright creditors' attorneys can sometimes find their way around those exemptions. You must also have a plan to continue payments on the loan in the event that your bank accounts are frozen by a creditor or else the loan will go into default and the lender will take your financial product to satisfy the loan. Calling in your loan and ultimately releasing the UCC-1 lien will cause your accounts receivables to once again be exposed to creditors, at precisely the wrong time. A good overall strategy that addresses these concerns within your overall business and estate plan structuring is a necessity.

Even within financial products it is critically important that your advisor can understand and review with you the products that have been suggested to you to purchase with the loan proceeds. Some products may dramatically outperform other products in your particular situation or address some of your specific business or estate planning needs. You simply cannot allow yourself to be crammed into a canned situation or else you may wake up a decade later only to figure out that the basic idea was a good one but it failed because the financial product employed was not the right one for you.

The documents provided to you by the lender will be the most important documents in the entire transaction because they will dictate when and how the lender can pull your puppet-strings in the deal. You will need an advisor who will carefully review the loan documents line-by-line to make sure the terms are not onerous and there are no hidden legal or tax traps for you to fall into. On this latter point, if the interest on the loan is deductible then the program will be much more efficient, but you will need tax advice on a very high level to make sure that any "tax bang" is correctly and optimally structured for you and your business interests.

There can also be significant differences between lenders and program administrators. Some are experienced and may understand your goals while others are inexperienced and may not understand all the issues involved. This is particularly true as accounts receivable financing becomes more and more of a mainstream planning tool and additional players try to jump into the game. Also, different lenders offer different rates on different terms and different program administrators have different deals worked out with the insurance companies who sell the financial products that facilitate these programs. You need an advisor who knows who offers the better programs and can compare and appraise their offerings to see which one is right for you.

Again, accounts receivable financing can be a wonderful and powerful tool or it can be a nightmare. Which one is for you depends on whether you allow yourself to be forced into a canned program; whether you will have an insurance agent who will conscientiously work hard to get you the best quotes and best products; and, whether you will have a tax or business planning attorney involved who can carefully review the arrangement against your overall business and personal planning and then line-by-line dissect the loan documents to make the agreements palatable to you and potentially expose hidden legal and tax traps.

Additional Information

More information about accounts receivable financing, including news & updates, overviews of some programs, cases, and similar supporting information, can be found on my "Financing Accounts Receivable" website at http://www.farbook.com

This website also has my current contact information and a form whereby you can ask me questions about various aspects of A/R financing. You can also e-mail me at ron@farbook.com or call me at 866-359-8851.

I am available to directly assist business owners in designing, comparing, and implementing their accounts receivable financing programs. I also am available to consult with insurance agents, financial planners, business consultants, attorneys, and others in designing and comparing accounts receivable plans for the use of their clients.

For those interested in asset protection issues, I would strongly suggest the free newsletter "Developments in Asset Protection and Wealth Preservation" published by the law firm of Riser Adkisson LLP as found at http://www.risad.com

Lexicon

Accounts Receivable—A line item on the balance sheet that shows the amount of money owed to the company from the sale of the company's products or services which have not yet been paid.

Accumulation Units—The value of the policyholder's interest in a variable annuity product expressed in units in the investment fund.

Accumulation Phase—The period when an annuity is being funded

Administrative fees—For recordkeeping and other administrative expenses

Annual Reset—Compares the change in the index from the beginning to the end of each year. Annual declines are ignored. Gains are 'locked-in' each year.

Annuitant—A person to whom the annuity is payable

Annuity—A contract that provides an income benefit for the life of a person, for the lives of two or more persons, or for a specified period of time.

Annuity Unit—The number of shares the annuitant will receive from a variable annuity account after the accumulation period ends and the benefits begin.

Annuitization Phase—The pay-out period for an annuity.

Asset Freeze—The process of getting assets to the children or the children's trust, so that the assets and their future growth are not exposed to the parent's creditors. This is the asset protection variant of the Estate Freeze.

Asset Protection Consultant—An unlicensed planner who fancies himself a lawyer and engages in asset protection planning outside of any attorney client privilege.

Asset Protection Kits—Do-it-yourself packages that purport to allow purchasers to create one-size-fits-all asset protection plans. Suffice it to say that the quality of these plans is highly suspect, which is compounded by the fact that the purchasers almost never implement the plans correctly anyhow, often leading to very negative tax consequences.

Badges of Fraud—In the fraudulent transfer context, a historically recognized non-exclusive list of circumstances that tend to show that the debtor intended to make a transfer in derogation of the rights of creditors.

Balance Sheet—Accounting statement showing the financial condition of a company at a particular date. Listed on the statement are the company's assets and liabilities, and capital and surplus.

Beneficiary—Designation by the owner of a life insurance policy indicating to whom the proceeds are to be paid upon the insured's death or when an endowment matures. *See also* Revocable Beneficiary and Irrevocable Beneficiary.

Benefit—Monetary sum paid or payable to a recipient for which the insurance company has received the premiums.

Beneficiary Taxed Irrevocable Trust (BETIR)—A trust set-up for you by some third person (such as a parent or sibling) with the client as the beneficiary and which is drafted so as to be treated as a grantor trust for federal income tax purposes.

Collateral—An asset which is used to guarantee a loan or indebtedness.

Cash Surrender Value—amount available to the owner when a life insurance policy is surrendered to the company.

Cash Value—the equity amount or savings accumulated in a whole life policy

Charging Order—An order issued by a court to a judgment creditor which essentially compels an entity of which the debtor is a partner or member to direct to the creditor until the judgment is satisfied any distributions that would otherwise have been made to the debtor.

Charging Order Protected Entities (COPEs)—Entities that restrict the remedies of a creditor of an owner to a "charging order" that entitles the creditor to distributions made in respect of that ownership interest, but do not allow—at least initially—the creditor to actually take the ownership interest. From an asset protection standpoint, the advantage is obvious: The creditor has no immediate means of getting at the assets in the entity even though the creditor holds a judgment against one of the owners.

Charging Order Protection—This prevents a creditor of an owner of particular types of business interests from reaching the assets of the business and from gaining voting control over the business interest. Rather, the creditor can only get a court order charging the debtor's interest with the debt, meaning that the creditor will receive any distributions made in respect of the debtor's interest. If the person in charge of making such distributions never makes one, the creditor may be out of luck. Originally, this protection arose to protect nondebtor partners from the debts of other partners of a business enterprise. Typically, the availability of charging order protection is limited to partnerships and limited liability companies, which is why Family Limited Partnerships are a popular asset protection tool.

Check-the-Box Regulations—Regulations promulgated by the Secretary of the Treasury in 1996 which allow an LLC simply to choose whether to be taxed as a partnership or a corporation.

Collateral Assignment—the assignment of a policy to a creditor as security for a debt. The creditor is entitled to be reimbursed for the amount of the owed and the beneficiary is entitled to any excess of the policy proceeds over the amount due the creditor in the event of the insured's death.

Combo Platter—A widely-marketed cookie-cutter asset protection structure involving an FLP with the limited partnership interests owned by a FAPT. The strategy is that if a creditor attacks the FLP, the FLP is liquidated into the FAPT and all assets moved offshore.

Cookie-Cutter Plan—A plan of a one-size-fits-all nature sold by promoters, who make enormous profits from selling such plans because their costs to implement the plan are nominal. The effectiveness of such plans is highly questionable, since typically if a creditor is able to defeat one plan then all similar plans can be likewise defeated.

Corporate Shell (a/k/a Corporate Veil)—Slang for the liability limiting advantage of a corporation, which limits the liability of shareholders to the equity they have contributed.

Corporation—A fictitious legal entity authorized by statute, created by the filing of Articles of Incorporation with the relevant jurisdiction, and capitalized by issuing shares of stock. A corporation can provide protection to the shareholders against the liabilities created by the corporation in excess of the corporation's capital.

Corridor—the space created between the total death benefit and the cash value of a Universal Life Insurance policy. An automatic increase in the death benefit results when the cash value approaches the initial face amount. If the space did not exist, the policy would not qualify for favorable tax treatment by the IRS.

Death Benefit—amount payable, as stated in the insurance policy, upon the death of the insured. This is the face value of the policy

Debt Financing—The financing of an entity by borrowing or by issuing bonds or promissory notes, etc. From an asset protection standpoint, the advantage of debt financing to equity financing is that in the event of a bankruptcy the debt-holders should have priority over general creditors of the entity in the distribution of the entity's assets.

Defense-In-Depth—A strategy whereby multiple layers of defenses are created with the idea that even though the creditor might ultimately be able to break through each layer, the creditor will eventually be worn down and settlement will be facilitated.

Deferred Annuity—An annuity where the annuity payments are delayed to some future date. Payments may be as a single premium payment or a series of installments.

Defined Benefit Plan—A pension plan under which benefits are determined by a specific benefit formula and contributions vary.

Defined Contribution Plan—A tax-qualified retirement plan in which annual contributions are determined by a formula set for those in the plan and the benefits vary.

Devaluation Strategy—A method of setting a low value for an asset by repeated sales to third-parties at successively lower prices, and which may include dissembling an asset with the idea of later reassembling it with the target purchaser.

Dilution Strategy—A method of decreasing a creditor's share or interest in an entity by issuing additional shares or interests to non-creditor shareholders or members.

Directors' and Officers' Liability (a/k/a D&O Liability)—The direct, personal liability of directors' and officers' of corporations for their acts that adversely affect the corporation (and thus giving rise to a shareholders' derivative action) and for the corporation's acts which adversely affect others (as in the case of employment discrimination claims).

Discretionary Trusts—A trust that allows the trustee the discretion to make or not make distributions of benefits to the beneficiary, and to make unequal distributions among all beneficiaries.

Disregarded Entity—An entity for which the tax consequences are attributed to its owner as if it did not exist, usually referring to a single-member limited liability company.

Doctrine of Disbelief—This doctrine holds that since no sane person would transfer all of their assets to a foreign trustee and risk the assets disappearing, it then stands to reason that they still retain some hidden control over the assets whether they admit to such control or not.

Domestic Asset Protection Trust (DAPT)—A self-settled spendthrift trust formed in a U.S. state that permits such forms of trust.

Dynasty Trust—A trust formed in a jurisdiction that has either abolished the Rule Against Perpetuities (which limits the duration of trusts) or has statutorily expanded the Rule Against Perpetuities for a period in excess of 100 years.

Employee Stock Ownership Plan (ESOP)—A plan formed to benefit and incentivize the employees of a business, and which can qualify for advantageous tax treatment.

Equity Indexed Annuity—A fixed deferred annuity that offers the traditional guaranteed minimum interest and an excess interest feature that is based on the performance of an equity market index, such as the S & P-500, etc.

Equity Stripping—The process of borrowing against an asset so as to reduce the debtor's equity in the asset.

ERISA—Employee Retirement Income Security Act of 1974—law that established rules and regulations to govern private pension plans, including vesting requirements, funding mechanisms, and general plan design and description.

ERISA Anti-Alienation Provision—A provision found in the Employee Retirement Security Act (ERISA) that prohibits a participant in an ERISA-qualified trust from transferring his or her interest in the plan to others, and which effectively prevents a creditor from attacking the assets of the plan while they are in the trust.

ESOP—(Employee Stock Ownership Plan)—A structure by which employees obtain shares in the company.

Estate Freeze—The process of transferring assets to either the children or a trust for the benefit of the children now, so that the future growth of those assets is with the children or their trust, and not within the parent's estate. The asset protection equivalent is known as an "asset freeze".

Estate Planning—Procedure for accumulating, conserving and distributing personal wealth.

Evidence of Insurability—Documentation of physical fitness by an applicant for insurance

Face Amount—The principle sum in the insurance contract. Actual payment may be decreased because of loans or increased by additional benefits payable under specified conditions.

Factoring—The process of selling the accounts receivable for immediate cash to a "Factor" who takes on the responsibility for collecting the receivable for a fee.

Family Limited Partnership (FLP)—A limited partnership which holds the family's business or investments, with the idea that the parents will gift interests in the partnership to their children at a discount, thus potentially saving federal gift and estate taxes. The term is planner's slang, since there is no entity called a "family limited partnership" that is referenced by any statute, nor is any such entity referenced in the Internal Revenue Code.

Federal Estate Tax—Federal tax imposed on the estate of a decedent according to the value of that estate

Fixed Annuity—A type of annuity that provides a guaranteed fixed benefit amount payable for the life of the annuitant.

Fraudulent Transfer (a/k/a "Fraudulent Conveyance")—A transfer in derogation of the rights of a creditor to satisfy his judgment against the assets of the debtor.

General Partnership (GP)—A partnership that consist only of general partners, all of who are jointly liable for the liabilities of the partnership, and all of whom have management rights to the partnership. In asset protection planning, general partnerships are usually to be avoided.

High Water Mark—Looks at the index value at various points during the contract, usually annual anniversaries. It then takes the highest of these values and compares it to the index level at the start of the term.

Homestead Exemption (a/k/a "Homestead Protection")—A statutory exemption against collection given to certain interests in real property being used as the primary residence of the debtor.

Immediate Annuity—Payments start immediately after premium is paid

Index Averaging—Average an index's value either daily or monthly rather than use the actual value of the index on a specified date. Averaging may reduce the amount of index-linked interest you can earn.

Indexed Whole Life Insurance—Policy with a face value that varies according to a prescribed index of prices, such as the Consumer Price Index (CPI)

Indexing Methods—Methods to determine the change in the relevant index over the period of the annuity. These varying methods impact the calculation of the amount of interest to be credited based on a change in the index. *See also* **Annual Reset**, **High Water Mark**, **Point-to-Point**, **Index Averaging**

Installment Refund Annuity—An income option in an annuity that provides for the funds remaining at the annuitant's death to be paid to the beneficiary in the form of continued annuity payments.

Interest Rate Cap—Upper limit on the maximum possible interest rate an insurance company will pay.

Interest Rate Caps—Some EIAs may put a cap or upper limit on your return. This cap rate is generally stated as a percentage. This is the maximum rate of interest the annuity will earn. For example, if the index linked to the annuity gained 10% and the cap rate was 8%, then the gain in the annuity would be 8%.

International Private Annuity Contract (IPAC)—A form of private annuity arrangement where the obligor to whom assets are sold and who will make the annuity payments is a foreign party domiciled in a tax and debtor haven jurisdiction.

Irrevocable Beneficiary—Beneficiary can be changed by the policyowner only with the written permission of that beneficiary

Irrevocable Life Insurance Trust (ILIT)—An irrevocable trust formed for the children, primarily to purchase and hold life insurance outside the parent's estate so that the life insurance proceeds are not subject to federal estate taxes at the parent's death.

Joint-And-Last-Survivor Annuity—Annuity that continues income payments as long as one annuitant, out of two or more annuitants, remains alive.

Joint-And-Last-Survivor Insurance—Coverage for two or more persons with the death benefit payable at the death of the last of those insured.

Joint-Life Annuity—Income payments continue until the death of the first of two or more annuitants.

Joint-Life Insurance—Coverage of two or more persons with the death benefit payable at the first death.

Keogh Plan (HR-10)—Permits self-employed individuals to establish his or her own retirement plan.

Laddering—The staggering of annuity start dates so that one annuity stream starts as another begins, or streams progressively start to increase the income to the annuitant.

Leveraging—The use of an asset as collateral, in addition its normal non-collateral uses.

LIBOR—London Interbank Operating Rate—a floating rate similar to the US prime rate.

Life Insurance—Insurance against the loss due to death of a particular person (the insured) upon whose death the insurance company agrees to pay a stated sum or income to the beneficiary.

Limited Liability Company (LLC)—A hybrid type of legal entity that combines certain traits of corporations with certain other traits of partnerships and other noncorporate legal entities. LLCs allow their owners (called members) to have the best of all worlds: pass-through tax treatment like a partnership, limited liability like a corporation, unheralded flexibility in ownership and management structure, and charging order protection.

Limited Partnership (LP)—A partnership that consist of general partners who are jointly liable for the liabilities of the partnership and who have management rights to the partnership, and limited partners whose liability is limited to their contributions to the partnership and who have no management rights, i.e., general partners are true partners and limited partners are mere passive investors.

Living Trust—A revocable grantor trust. Because the trust can be revoked, and a court can order a settlor to revoke the trust, the living trust is thought not to provide any meaningful asset protection until the death of the settlor.

Management Company—A company formed primarily to act as a manager of another entity, distance control of the other entity from the owners, and absorb liabilities arising from the management function.

Manager-Managed LLC (MemLLC)—An LLC that provides for one or more designated managers to have management rights, and with the members having no management rights. With a Member Managed LLC, the members are in a role very similar to limited partners.

Member-Managed LLC (MgrLLC)—An LLC that allows the members to have management rights, very similar in operation to a general partnership, but with some degree of limited liability for the members.

Modified Endowment Contract (MEC)—The characterization of a life insurance policy for tax purposes that would allow, among other benefits, tax-free loans against cash value.

Mortality and Expense Charges—The insurance company charges for the insurance risk it takes under the contract

NAIC—National Association of Insurance Commissioners—Association of state insurance commissioners active in the formation and recommendations of uniform regulations and legislation pertaining to all insurance matters. www.naic.org

NASD—National Association of Securities Dealers—Association which, among other things, regulates and enforces issues involving variable insurance products www.nasd.org

Non-Qualified Plan—A retirement plan that does not meet the federal governments requirements and is not eligible for favorable tax treatment.

Paid-Up Policy—No further premiums are to be paid to receive the benefits promised by the insurance company

Participation Rates—A participation rate determines how much of the gain in the index will be credited to the annuity. For example, the insurance company may set the participation rate at 80%, which means the annuity would only be credited with 80% of the gain experienced by the index

Partnership—A partnership is an association of two or more persons carrying on a business venture as co-owners for profit. Partnerships come in two basic varieties: general and limited.

Payment Certain—Phrase used to describe a method of annuity payout that guarantees a specified number of years, regardless of whether an annuitant remains alive.

***Per Stirpes* Rule**—The death proceeds from an insurance policy are to be divided equally among the named beneficiaries; however, if a named beneficiary is deceased, his or her share then goes to the living descendents of that individual.

Piercing the Corporate Veil—Where a court disregards the legal fiction of the corporation and imposes liability against the shareholders.

Point-to-Point—Compares the change in the index at two discrete points in time, such as the beginning and ending dates of the contract term.

Policy Loan—A loan made by the insurance company to the policyowner with the policy's cash value assigned as security

Pre-Bankruptcy Planning—Planning that is done immediately in anticipation of a bankruptcy filing, and which seeks to maximize exemptions and avoid claims of preferential transfers.

Preferential Transfer—A transfer that has the effect of alienating property in advance of a bankruptcy filing, and which may usually be set aside by the bankruptcy court within a defined time period.

Private Annuity—A method of selling an asset whereby the seller (obligee) sells the asset to the buyer (obligor) in exchange for the buyer agreeing to make certain payments to the seller until the seller dies. To qualify as a Private Annuity for U.S. tax purposes, in addition to other requirements, the buyer (obligor) must not be in the business of issuing annuities.

Professional Corporation (PC)—A form of corporation that can have only certain licensed professionals as shareholders, and which typically does not protect the professional shareholder from lawsuits brought alleging their professional negligence.

Program Facilitator—A professional company that specializes in accounts receivable financing. The Program Facilitator generally qualifies the applicant, develops the pro forma program analysis and acts on behalf of the lender.

Promoter—One who sells one-size-fits-all cookie-cutter plans to any client whose check clears, regardless of whether the plan is suitable for the particular client or not. Promoters often attempt to maximize their profits by selling asset protection kits.

Pure Trust—A sham trust sold by scam artists that purports to be free of government regulation, taxation, or intervention because of the Contract Clause of the U.S. Constitution.

Purpose Trust—A form of trust which has no beneficiaries, but instead exists to serve some purpose such as to benefit cancer research. Because the trust has no beneficiaries, it is sometimes used in the asset protection context for holding title to management companies.

Qualified Plan—A retirement or employee compensation plan maintained by an employer that meets specific IRS guidelines and receives favorable tax treatment.

Reverse Alter Ego—A developing theory of relief for creditors, which allows creditors of an owner of an entity to invade the entity and get at the entity's assets directly so as to satisfy the creditor's debt against the owner.

Revocable Beneficiary—Beneficiary can be changed by policyowner at any time

Self-Canceling Installment Note (SCIN)—A method of selling an asset where the buyer provides a promissory note to the seller with a fixed payment period, but which note and obligation to pay the seller is canceled if the seller dies.

Self-Settled Spendthrift Trust—A trust formed for the benefit of the person who created the trust, with spendthrift provisions that attempt to disallow a creditor from invading the trust assets or forcing a distribution to the beneficiary that the creditor would then seize.

Series LLC (a/k/a "Cell LLC")—A form of LLC allowed by the statutes of only a few jurisdictions (most popularly Delaware) that allow membership interests to be divided into categories or "cells" with liability for particular actions of the LLC theoretically limited to the capital contributed to the particular series in which the operations of the LLC occurred.

Settlor—One who provides assets to a trustee, so that the trustee can hold the assets in trust for the beneficiary.

Single-Member LLC (SMLLC)—An LLC with but one member, who is typically also the manager, formed in a jurisdiction that allows a single member. Because they are relatively untested, the liability protections of SMLLCs are mostly theoretical, but should be similar to that of a sole-shareholder corporation.

Special features—Such as stepped-up death benefit or a guaranteed minimum income benefit

Spendthrift Provisions—(as used in insurance) stipulates that, to the extent permitted by law, policy proceeds shall not be subject to the claims of creditors of the beneficiary or policyowner.

Spendthrift Trusts—A trust that includes certain language giving the trustee wide latitude to avoid making distributions to beneficiaries where the distribution would go to a creditor, or where the trustee fears the distribution would be wasted by the beneficiary.

Single Premium Immediate Annuity (SPIA)—An annuity that is funded with a single premium and annuitization is immediate.

Single Premium Deferred Annuity (SPDA)—An annuity that is funded with a single premium but annuitization is to be determined at a later date.

Spread/Margin/Asset Fee—Some EIAs use a spread, margin or asset fee in addition to, or instead of, a participation rate. This percentage will be subtracted from any gain in the index linked to the annuity. For example, if the index gained 10% and the spread/margin/asset fee is 3.5%, then the gain in the annuity would be only 6.5%.

Standard & Poor's 500 (S&P-500)—Commonly used index that represents a broad cross-section of common stock traded on the New York Stock Exchange, the American Stock Exchange and NASDAQ. This index is a selection of 500 leading companies from 100 distinct industry groups found in 10 leading industry sectors. These sectors include energy, industrials, health care, utilities, communication services, etc.

Structural Methodology—The decision-making process for choosing the type of structure that will be utilized hold particular assets.

Structured Financial Product—A financial product created to serve a transaction-specific purpose.

Surrender Charge—Fee that you owe if you withdraw money from the annuity before a specified period

Tax Sheltered Annuity (TSA)—An annuity plan reserved for nonprofit organizations and their employees. Funds contributed to the annuity are excluded from current taxable income and are only taxed later when benefits are paid. Also called a tax-deferred annuity and 403(b) plan.

Term Life Insurance—Provides coverage for a specified and limited period of time (the "term"). Premiums for most term policies increase with age or at the end of each renewal period. After the policy or term ends, there is no benefit payment if the insured person survives beyond the policy period.

Transfer Methodology—The decision-making process for choosing the type of transfer that will be used to move assets to a particular structure.

Trust—A relationship whereby one party (trustee) is given assets by another (settlor) to hold for the benefit of a third party (beneficiary).

Trust Protector—A person or entity who has certain powers under the trust document, usually to discharge (but not appoint) trustees, and to veto (but not make) certain key decisions of the trustees.

Trustee—One who agrees with a settlor to hold assets in trust for the beneficiary.

UCC-1—A lien filed with the county clerk's office on a consumer good or commercial instrument, much like a home mortgage. UCC stands for the Uniform Commercial Code and the form is National UCC Financing Statement.

Unbundling—The process of breaking an asset into components and treating the components as separate assets.

Uniform Fraudulent Transfers Act (UFTA)—A statute that sets forth the fraudulent transfer laws of most states.

Universal Life Insurance—Can also provide coverage for the life of the insured while at the same time providing flexibility in premium payments and in insurance coverage. The cost of insurance protection and, in some cases, other costs are deducted from the cash or policy account value

Variable Annuity—Annuity in which premium payments are used to purchase accumulation units, the value of which are determined by the value of the portfolio of stocks in which the insurance company invests the premiums. The owner assumes the risk for the performance of various investment options made available by the insurance company.

Variable Life Insurance—A variation of whole life insurance which offers a fixed premium schedule and a minimum death benefit. But it differs from traditional whole life insurance in that cash values are invested in portfolios of securities in an account separate from the general assets of the insurance company. A policyholder has discretion in choosing the mix of investments the policy offers. The insurance company does not guarantee investment returns and your cash value will fluctuate.

Variable Universal Life Insurance—Combines features of universal life insurance and variable life insurance

Wealth Preservation—Planning that preserves wealth over time against numerous unforeseen circumstances.

Whole Life Insurance—Or "ordinary life insurance" is a form of permanent life insurance. This means it can provide coverage for the life of the insured. It also can build cash value, which is a savings feature. Premium payments typically remain level for the life of the insured.

Zero-Coupon Bond—Typically, a bond that has been stripped of its interest coupons so that only a single lump-sum payment is made at maturity.

Appendix A

National Association of Insurance Commissioners (NAIC)

Consumer Alert
Tips for Buying Life Insurance

Life insurance is an important purchase for most Americans because it can provide income replacement to beneficiaries in the event of a death. Life insurance policies are available from more than 2,000 life insurance companies in the United States. Here are some tips from the National Association of Insurance Commissioners (NAIC) to help you get the best value for your life insurance dollar.

1. Review Your Insurance Needs

Choose the kind of policy that has benefits that most closely fit your needs. Consider the number of people who are dependent upon you financially and whether or not you need life insurance. Will you have substantial debts and taxes owed after your death? Do you have alternatives to life insurance, such as savings accounts or other investments that could take care of expenses after your death?

2. Know Your Options

There are two basic types of life insurance: term insurance and cash-value insurance. You may wish to combine cash-value life insurance with term insurance for the period of your greatest need for life insurance to replace income. Make sure the price is right. If the premium increases later and you still need insurance, will you be able to afford it?

3. Comparison Shop

Life insurance is a competitive marketplace, and much of the competition focuses on price. After you have decided which kind of life insurance is best for you, compare similar policies from different companies to find which one is likely to give you the best value for your money.

4. Know Your Company

You can check the financial stability of any life insurance company through several reputable national rating companies. Some of these ratings are available at public libraries. Check with your state insurance department to verify that the company is authorized to do business in your state.

5. Read Your Policy Carefully before Signing

Never buy a policy you don't understand—if you are given illustrations or booklets, save these materials with your policy. Make sure you understand the guarantees in your policy and the surrender penalties if you choose to drop the policy at any time. Ask your agent or company about anything that is not clear to you.

6. Regularly Review Your Policy; Update Accordingly

Review your life insurance program with your agent or company every few years to keep up with changes in your income and your needs. This includes a review of your net worth to reconsider the prospects your survivors may face when you pass away.

7. Consider Replacement Cost

It may be costly to replace your insurance if you change your mind during the early years of the policy. Don't drop one policy and buy another without a thorough study of the new policy and the one you currently have.

8. Get More Information

For further information, order a copy of the "Life Insurance Buyer's Guide" from the NAIC at www.naic.org. If you believe you have been treated unfairly in shopping for life insurance, please contact your state insurance department. You can link to your insurance department's Web site by visiting www.naic.org. After clicking on "State Insurance Web Sites," click on your state.

The National Association of Insurance Commissioners is a voluntary organization of the chief insurance regulatory officials of the 50 states, the District of Columbia and four U.S. territories. The overriding objectives of state regulators are to protect consumers and help maintain the financial stability of the insurance industry. If you would like more information, please contact the NAIC Communications Department at (816) 842-3600 or send e-mail to communications@naic.org.

APPENDIX B

National Association of Insurance Commissioners (NAIC)

Consumer Alert
Protect Yourself: Avoid Deceptive Sales Practices

You buy insurance to protect yourself or your loved ones financially from illness, automobile accidents, house fires or death. However, if you become the victim of deceptive sales practices and the insurance you buy isn't legitimate, you have not only wasted the money you paid for premiums, but could face hundreds or thousands of dollars in unpaid claims. Here are some tips from the National Association of Insurance Commissioners (NAIC) to protect yourself from becoming a victim of deceptive insurance sales practices.

1. What are Deceptive Sales Practices?

Inappropriate sales practices, or the deliberate deception of a consumer, can occur in any line of insurance, including auto, homeowners, health, life, worker's compensation and medical malpractice. Companies or agencies may sell illegal products or policies through direct-mail solicitations, newspaper or magazine advertisements or over the Internet. Anyone can be a victim of deceptive sales practices. But, with a few measures, you can protect yourself.

2. Verify the Company and Agent

In order to sell insurance in your state, companies and agents must be licensed. To confirm the credibility of a company or agent, contact your state insurance department, and ask the following questions:

- Is the company licensed in your state?

- Is the company licensed to sell the line of insurance you are interested in purchasing?
- Is the agent licensed in your state and a legitimate representative of the company?
- Does the company have a good record of handling complaints?
- Have any complaints been filed against the agent?

3. Check Their Credit Rating

Legitimate insurers have their "creditworthiness" rated by independent agencies such as Standard & Poor's, A.M. Best Co. or Moody's Investors Services. An "A+++" or "AAA" rating is a sign of a company's strong financial stability. You can check a company's rating online or at your local library.

4. The Proof is in the Paperwork

As you complete your research and decide to purchase a particular policy, it's important to keep detailed records. Get all rate quotes and key information in writing. Also, once you've decided to make a purchase, keep a copy of all paperwork you complete and sign, as well as any correspondence, special offers and payment receipts.

Please note: You should receive a copy—not a photocopy—of your new policy within 30 to 60 days of purchase. If you do not receive your copy, contact the insurance company or agent immediately.

5. Insurance "Red Flags"

Watch for these "red flags" that could warn you of possible deceptive sales practices:

- High-pressure sales pitch. If a particular group or agent has contacted you repeatedly, offering a "limited-time" offer that makes you uncomfortable or aggravated, trust your instincts and steer clear.
- Quick-change tactics. Skilled scam artists will try to prey on your "time fears." They may try to convince you to change coverage quickly without giving you the opportunity to do adequate research.
- Unwilling or unable to prove credibility. A licensed agent will be more than willing to show adequate credentials.
- If it seems too good to be true, it probably is!

6. Get More Information

Your state insurance department is your best source for information on company and agent requirements, as well as available products. If you suspect you've been a victim of deceptive sales practices, report it to your state insurance department. You can link to your state insurance department's Web site by visiting www.naic.org. Click on "State Insurance Web Sites," then click on your state.

The National Association of Insurance Commissioners is a voluntary organization of the chief insurance regulatory officials of the 50 states, the District of Columbia and four U.S. territories. The overriding objectives of state regulators are to protect consumers and help maintain the financial stability of the insurance industry. If you would like more information, please contact the NAIC Communications Department at (816) 842-3600 or send e-mail to communications@naic.org.

APPENDIX C

National Association of Securities Dealers (NASD) Investor Alert Equity-Indexed Annuities—A Complex Choice

Updated: June 30, 2005

Why an Alert on Equity-Indexed Annuities?

Sales of **equity-indexed annuities (EIAs)** have grown considerably in recent years. Although one insurance company includes the word "simple" in the name of their product, EIAs are anything but easy to understand. One of the confusing features of an EIA is the method used to calculate the gain in the index to which the annuity is linked. To make matters worse, there are not one, but several different indexing methods. Because of the variety and complexity of the methods used to credit interest, investors will find it difficult to compare one EIA to another.

Before you buy an EIA, you should understand the various features of this investment and be prepared to ask your insurance agent, broker, financial planner, or other financial professional lots of questions about whether an EIA is right for you.

What is an Annuity?

An annuity is a contract between you and an insurance company in which the company promises to make periodic payments to you, starting immediately or at some future date. If the payments are delayed to the future, you have a **deferred annuity**. If the payments start immediately, you have an **immediate annuity**. You buy the annuity either with a single payment or a series of payments called premiums.

Annuities come in two types: fixed and variable. With a **fixed annuity**, the insurance company guarantees both the rate of return and the payout. As its name implies, a **variable annuity's** rate of return is not stable, but varies with the stock, bond, and money market funds that you choose as investment options. There is no guarantee that you will earn any return on your investment and there is a risk that you will lose money. Unlike fixed contracts, variable annuities are securities registered with the Securities Exchange Commission (SEC). To learn more about variable annuities, read our Investor Alert, Should You Exchange Your Variable Annuity?

What is an Equity-Indexed Annuity?

EIAs have characteristics of both fixed and variable annuities. Their return varies more than a fixed annuity, but not as much as a variable annuity. So EIAs give you more risk (but more potential return) than a fixed annuity but less risk (and less potential return) than a variable annuity.

EIAs offer a minimum guaranteed interest rate combined with an interest rate linked to a market index. Because of the guaranteed interest rate, EIAs have less market risk than variable annuities. EIAs also have the potential to earn returns better than traditional fixed annuities when the stock market is rising.

What is the Guaranteed Minimum Return?

The guaranteed minimum return for an EIA is typically 90% of the premium paid at a 3% annual interest rate. However, if you surrender your EIA early, you may have to pay a significant surrender charge and a 10% tax penalty that will reduce or eliminate any return.

How good is this guarantee?

Your guaranteed return is only as good as the insurance company that gives it. While it is not a common occurrence that a life insurance company is unable to meet its obligations, it happens. There are several private companies that rate an insurance company's financial strength. Information about these firms can be found on the New Jersey Department of Banking & Insurance's Web site.

What is a market index?

A market index tracks the performance of a specific group of stocks representing a particular segment of the market, or in some cases an entire market. For example, S&P 500 Composite Stock Price Index is an index of 500 stocks intended to be representative of a broad segment of the market. There are indexes for almost every conceivable sector of the stock market. Most EIAs are based on the S&P 500, but other indexes also are used. Some EIAs even allow investors to select one or more indexes.

How is an EIA's index-linked interest rate compounded?

The index-linked gain depends on the particular combination of indexing features that an EIA uses. The most common indexing features are listed below. To fully understand an EIA, make sure you not only understand each feature, but also how the features work together since these features can dramatically impact the return on your investment.

- **Participation Rates.** A participation rate determines how much of the gain in the index will be credited to the annuity. For example, the insurance company may set the participation rate at 80%, which means the annuity would only be credited with 80% of the gain experienced by the index.

- **Spread/Margin/Asset Fee.** Some EIAs use a spread, margin or asset fee in addition to, or instead of, a participation rate. This percentage will be subtracted from any gain in the index to the annuity. For example, if the index gained 10% and the spread/margin/asset fee is 3.5%, then the gain in the annuity would only be 6.5%.

- **Interest Rate Caps.** Some EIAs may put a cap or upper limit on your return. This cap rate is generally stated as a percentage. This is the maximum rate of interest the annuity will earn. For example, if the indeed linked to the annuity gained 10% and the cap rate was 8%, then the gain in the annuity would be 8%.

Caution! Some EIAs allow the insurance company to change participation rates, cap rates, or spread/margin/asset fees either annually or at the start of the next contract term. If an insurance company subsequently lowers the participation rate or cap rate or increases the spread/margin/asset fees, this could adversely affect you return. Read you contract carefully to see if it allows the insurance company to change these features.

Indexing Methods. As described in the table below, there are several methods for determining the change in the relevant index over the period of the annuity. These varying methods impact the calculation of the amount of interest to be credited to the contract based on a change in the index.

Indexing Method	Description
Annual Reset	Compares the change in the index from the beginning to the end of each year. Any declines are ignored.
	Advantage: Your gain is "locked in" each year
	Disadvantage: Can be combined with other features, such as lower cap rates and participation rates that will limit the amount of interest you might gain each year.
High Water Mark	Looks at the index value at various points during the contract, usually annual anniversaries. It then takes the highest of these values and compares it to the index level at the start of the term.
	Advantage: May credit you with more interest than other indexing methods and protect against declines in the index.
	Disadvantage: Because interest is not credited until the end of the term, you may not receive an index-link gain if you surrender your EIA early. It can also be combined with other features; such as lower cap rates and participation rates that will limit the amount of interest you might gain each year.
Point to Point	Compares the change in the index at two discrete points in time, such as the beginning and ending dates of the contract term.

> **Advantage:** May be combined with other features, such as higher cap and participation rates, that may credit you with more interest.
>
> **Disadvantage:** Relies on single point in time to calculate interest. Therefore, even if the index that your annuity is linked to is going up throughout the term of your investment, if it declines dramatically on the last day of the term, then part or all of the earlier gain can be lost. Because interest is not credited until the end of the term, you may not receive any index-link gain if you surrender your EIA early.

- **Index Averaging.** Some EIAs average an index's value either daily or monthly rather than use the actual value of the index on a specific date. Averaging may reduce the amount of index-linked interest you earn.

- **Interest Calculation.** The way that an insurance company calculates interest earned during the term of the EIA can make a big difference in the amount of money you will earn. Some EIAs pay simple interest during the term of the annuity. Because there is no compounding of interest, your return will be lower.

- **Exclusion of Dividends.** Most EIA only count equity index gains from market price gains, excluding any gains from dividends. Since you're not earning dividends, you won't earn as much as if you invested directly in the market.

Can I get my money back when I need it?

EIAs are long-term investments. Getting out early may mean taking a loss. Many EIAs have surrender charges. The surrender charge can be a percentage of the amount withdrawn or a reduction in the interest rate credited to the EIA.

Also, any withdrawals from tax-deferred annuities before you reach the age of 591/2 are generally subject to a 10% tax penalty in addition to any gain being taxed as ordinary income.

Do EIAs and other tax-deferred annuities provide the same advantages as 401(k) and other before tax retirement plans?

No, 401(k) plans and other before-tax retirement savings plans not only allow you to defer taxes on income and investment gains, but your contributions reduce your current taxable income. That's why most investors should consider an EIA and other annuity products only after they make the maximum contribution to their 401(k) and other before-tax retirement plans. To learn more about 401(k)s, please read *Smart 401(k) Investing.*

Is it possible to lose money in an EIA?

Yes. Many insurance companies only guarantee that you'll receive 90% of the premiums you paid, plus at least 3% interest. Therefore, if you don't receive any index-linked interest, you could lose money on your investment. One way that you could not receive any index-linked interest is if the index linked to your annuity declines. The other way you may not receive and index-linked interest is if you surrender your EIA before maturity. Some insurance companies will not credit you with index-linked interest when you surrender your annuity early.

If you have questions about EIAs, you can contact your state insurance commissioner. You can check out whether the person selling an EIA is registered with the NASD check their Web site or call their Hotline at 800-289-9999.

Appendix D

Securities Exchange Act of 1934

Section 11—Trading by Members of Exchanges, Brokers, and Dealers
d. Prohibition on extension of credit by broker-dealer

It shall be unlawful for a member of a national securities exchange who is both a dealer and a broker, or for any person who both as a broker and a dealer transacts a business in securities through the medium of a member or otherwise, to effect the use of any facility of a national securities exchange or of the mails or of any means or instrumentality of interstate commerce, or otherwise in the case of a member, (1) any transaction in connection with which, directly or indirectly, he extends or maintains or arranges for the extension or maintenance of credit to or for a customer on any security (other than exempted security) which was a part of a new issue in the distribution of which he participated as a member of a selling syndicate or group within thirty days prior to such transaction: Provided, That credit shall not be deemed extended by reason of a bona fide delayed delivery of (i) any such security against full payment of the entire purchase price thereof upon such delivery within thirty-five days after such purchase or (ii) any mortgage related security or any small business related security against full payment of the entire purchase price thereof upon such delivery by rule or regulation…

END

978-0-595-37044-3
0-595-37044-6